ROSE GUIDE TO THE
EPISTLES

R SE
PUBLISHING

Rose Guide to the Epistles
©2022 Rose Publishing

Published by Rose Publishing
An imprint of Tyndale House Ministries
Carol Stream, Illinois
www.hendricksonrose.com

ISBN 978-1-64938-022-7

Contributing author: Aaron W. White, PhD

Chapter six: *The Seven Churches of Revelation* (Rose Publishing, 2015); chapter seven: *Understanding the Book of Revelation* (Rose Publishing, 2009); "Why Did the Epistles Become Part of the New Testament?" adapted from *The Gospels: "Lost" & Found* by Timothy Paul Jones (Rose Publishing, 2007).

Relief map by Michael Schmeling/www.aridocean.com.
Photos used under license from Shutterstock.com.

Printed in the United States of America
010722VP

CONTENTS

CHAPTER 1

The Epistles: An Overview

Christians began writing letters to churches from the earliest days of Christianity. The newly planted congregations needed to know more about who Jesus was, especially since the four gospels about the life of Jesus were not written until the latter half of the first century. These letters were essential for instruction about what it meant to live out the Christian faith. Collected and grouped together in our Bible today, these letters are what we call the New Testament Epistles.

The word *epistle* comes from the Greek word *epistole,* which simply means "message, commission, or letter." The New Testament Epistles were sent to diverse and growing churches in the Mediterranean world and were written to address specific issues the churches faced. So when we read these epistles today, it is very literally reading someone else's mail.

Though penned two thousand years ago, these letters tackle topics that are still pressing issues for believers today: church diversity, holy living, false doctrines, ministry leadership, persecution, and how to find hope in the future return of Christ Jesus.

THE EPISTLE GENRE

The Bible has many different types of writings within its pages. Some of it is poetry, like the musical lyrics in the Psalms. Some writings are historical, like the epic narratives of Moses and the exodus, and others are wisdom literature, like the proverbs of wise King Solomon. Categories such as these are called *genre*. Much like we would sort music into categories of pop, rock, jazz, classical, or country, the books of the Bible can be sorted according to their genres.

Twenty-one of the twenty-seven books of the New Testament fit the ancient genre of epistle. This epistle genre is not a one-size-fits-all. In fact, some ancient sources list anywhere from twenty-one to forty-one different types of epistles. Although the New Testament Epistles do not follow any of these types exactly, the genre can take on various forms and does so in the New Testament.

WHO WROTE THE EPISTLES?

Paul

Of all the epistle authors, the apostle Paul stands out. His writings make up nearly half of the New Testament, which has led some historians to regard Paul not merely as a great writer of Scripture but also as one of the great letter writers in history. Thirteen of the twenty-one epistles were written by Paul.

The various roles Paul takes on in the book of Acts and in his epistles is quite staggering. We see him as a pastor, church planter, missionary, teacher, and in some cases, like a mother or father (see for example, 1 Cor. 4:17; Gal. 4:19–20; 1 Thess. 2:7–8; 2 Thess. 2:15–16). Paul's ministry was rich in character and broad in its reach, which makes sense if we consider his ministry philosophy of becoming "all things to all people so that by all possible means [he] might save some" (1 Cor. 9:22).

Peter and Paul by Guido Reni

What we know of Paul's life comes from Luke's writings in the book of Acts, where we find Paul's conversion story on the road to Damascus (Acts 9) and the extensive narratives of his missionary journeys (Acts 13–28). We also have a window into Paul's life when he mentions things about himself in his epistles, specifically Galatians 1:11–24 (he explains his prior status as a zealous persecutor of Christians) and Philippians 3:3–6 (his travels immediately after his conversion to Christianity).

Peter

Peter was one of Jesus' original twelve disciples, an eyewitness to the ministry of Christ. He became the most prominent leader of the early and rapidly growing church (see Acts 2). Information about Peter's life comes mostly from the first five books of the New Testament: Matthew, Mark, Luke, John, and Acts.

His two back-to-back epistles (1 and 2 Peter) were written late in his life, about thirty years after Christ. It is believed that not long after writing these letters, he was martyred in Rome under Emperor Nero's persecution of Christians.

John

Like Peter, John was one of the original twelve disciples and an eyewitness of Christ. John was a prolific writer, penning the gospel that bears his

John the Evangelist

name, the apocalyptic book of Revelation, and three epistles. While the gospel of John and Revelation are lengthy, the epistles of 1, 2, and 3 John are among the shortest books of the Bible.

Though John is not featured in the book of Acts as much as Peter or Paul, he nonetheless emerged as an important leader of the early church (see Acts 3–4). We learn about John's life from the Gospels, Acts, his letters, and the writings of other early church leaders such as Irenaeus and Polycarp. John is believed to have lived the longest of any of the twelve apostles, and he wrote his books late in his life. According to tradition, John died of natural causes in Ephesus near the end of the first century.

Other Writers

- Two of the epistles are believed to have been written by Jesus' brothers James and Jude.

- In four of Paul's epistles, he identifies Timothy, his fellow missionary traveler, as also sending the letter and possibly co-authoring them since Paul sometimes uses "we" instead of "I" in these letters (Phil. 1:1; Col. 1:1; 1 Thess. 1:1; 2 Thess. 1:1).

- Hebrews stands out as the only entirely anonymous letter. Various theories of its authorship have been proposed—Paul, Apollos, or Priscilla—but there are not enough clues in the letter to determine with any certainty who authored it.

Secretaries

Following a known Greco-Roman practice of using a secretary for writing, called an *amanuensis,* the New Testament authors often utilized individuals to compose their epistles. Paul is most known for using a secretary. At the end of the epistle to the Romans, Tertius identifies himself as the secretary of the letter: "I, Tertius, who wrote down this letter, greet you in the Lord" (Rom. 16:22). Sometimes Paul would add his autograph: "I, Paul, write this greeting in my own hand" (1 Cor. 16:21; Col. 4:18; 2 Thess. 3:17; Philem. 1:19). The freedom that Paul gave his secretary is debated, but the common way a secretary operated involved a degree of creative freedom. Secretaries would take notes of dictation and at times edit them; in other circumstances the secretaries were simply instructed to write about certain themes. Such freedom may be a reason why Paul appears to express himself in diverse ways throughout his letter-writing career.

Peter is also known to have used a secretary (1 Peter 5:12), and in some ways Mark was Peter's secretary when writing the gospel of Mark. The early church father Papias was told by the apostle John that Mark received anecdotes of the life of Jesus from Peter and edited them into a coherent order.

John dictates the book of Revelation to his secretary (Cave of the Apocalypse, Patmos)

HOW ARE THE EPISTLES ARRANGED?

Most church traditions have arranged the New Testament Epistles into three basic groups. Open your Bible and right after the book of Acts you will find the epistles written by Paul to various churches, followed by Paul's epistles to individuals, and then comes what are called the General Epistles, which are all the epistles *not* written by Paul. The epistles in these categories are arranged, more or less, by size, with the longer letters first and shorter ones near the end.

> ### THE PRISON EPISTLES
>
> The epistles of Ephesians, Philippians, Colossians, and Philemon are collectively called the Prison Epistles. Paul wrote these four letters around AD 60–62 from prison— or, more precisely, while guarded under house arrest in Rome, awaiting trial (Acts 28:16, 30).

Paul's Epistles to Churches

This first category includes the first nine epistles in the New Testament. These letters were written to churches for specific reasons. The letters are named after the congregations who received them, and they include Paul's letter to the Romans, his first and second letter to the Corinthians, Galatians, Ephesians, Philippians, Colossians, and the two letters to the Thessalonians. Romans and 1 Corinthians are Paul's longest epistles.

Paul's Epistles to Individuals

The second category includes Paul's four letters written to particular people. These include Paul's first and second letter to Timothy, his disciple and a young pastor; his letter to Titus, also a pastor; and his letter to a church leader named Philemon. Much like the epistles addressed to whole church congregations, even Paul's letters to individuals seem to have public appeal because they were circulated to various churches. The two letters to Timothy and Titus are often group together and called the Pastoral Epistles, since Paul is writing advice to pastors.

General Epistles

The General Epistles include the final eight letters in the New Testament. They are as follows: Hebrews, written by an anonymous author; and then James; 1 and 2 Peter; 1, 2, and 3 John; and Jude—each named after their author. Hebrews is the longest epistle and 3 John the shortest, though Jude also is quite a short letter.

Revelation

Revelation stands out as the most unique book of the New Testament. It is not a gospel—like Matthew, Mark, Luke, or John—nor does it fit the pattern of the epistles. However, it does begin like an epistle: "John, to the seven churches in the province of Asia" (Rev. 1:4). The first three chapters contain seven short letters to seven churches in Asia Minor (modern-day Turkey). The book of Revelation, however, is written as apocalyptic literature. In this type of writing in the Bible, God's hidden plans are revealed through visions, symbols, and images.

PAUL'S EPISTLES TO CHURCHES	PAUL'S EPISTLES TO INDIVIDUALS	GENERAL EPISTLES
Romans	1 Timothy	Hebrews
1 Corinthians	2 Timothy	James
2 Corinthians	Titus	1 Peter
Galatians	Philemon	2 Peter
Ephesians		1 John
Philippians		2 John
Colossians		3 John
1 Thessalonians		Jude
2 Thessalonians		

WHAT IS IN AN EPISTLE?

Just like there are certain expectations for how we should write a formal letter or email today, there were general expectations in the first century for how an epistle should be written. The New Testament Epistles have a basic structure of six components, though there are always exceptions to the rule.

1. Firstly, the author identifies himself.

In fact, the first word in all of Paul's letters is his name. Likewise, James, Jude, and Peter in their epistles identify themselves right away. John, who can tend to stand outside of convention, does not identify himself in his first epistle and calls himself "the elder" in his other two epistles (2 John 1:1; 3 John 1:1). Hebrews is another exception to this rule, where the writer skips this part of an epistle entirely.

SIX PARTS OF AN EPISTLE

1. Author
2. Recipient
3. Greeting
4. Body
5. Application
6. Closing Greetings

Along with the author's name, we sometimes find a claim to authority that would give him the right to send such a correspondence. Paul tends to be creative in his credentialing, calling himself "a prisoner of Christ" (Philem. 1:1) and "an apostle—sent … by Jesus Christ and God the Father" (Gal. 1:1). Similarly, Peter begins his first letter calling himself "an apostle of Jesus Christ" (1 Peter 1:1).

2. Next, the author identifies who he is writing to.

Paul often writes to believers in a particular city, as in his letter to the Colossians: "To God's holy people in Colossae" (Col. 1:2). But in other cases the letter is for several churches in a region, for example, "to the churches in Galatia" (Gal. 1:2). These were circular letters and were meant to travel the circuit, so to speak, being read to multiple congregations. Paul's shortest epistle is a personal appeal specifically addressed firstly "to Philemon our dear friend and fellow worker," and then "also to Apphia our sister and Archippus our fellow soldier"—possibly members of Philemon's household (Philem. 1:1–2). James, interestingly, addresses his letter "to the twelve tribes scattered among the nations," probably an allusion to Jewish Christians living outside Israel (James 1:1).

3. The author then gives a greeting.

The greeting may be quite general, though theologically rich, like we see in Galatians:

> Grace and peace to you from God our Father and the Lord Jesus Christ, who gave himself for our sins to rescue us from the present evil age, according to the will of our God and Father, to whom be glory for ever and ever. Amen.
>
> GALATIANS 1:3–5

It can be a single word, as seen in James:

> "Greetings."
>
> JAMES 1:1

But it can also be deeply personal and lengthy, like how Paul begins 2 Corinthians:

> Praise be to the God and Father of our Lord Jesus Christ, the Father of compassion and the God of all comfort, who comforts us in all our troubles, so that we can comfort those in any trouble with the comfort we ourselves receive from God. For just as we share abundantly in the sufferings of Christ, so also our comfort abounds through Christ. If we

are distressed, it is for your comfort and salvation; if we are comforted, it is for your comfort, which produces in you patient endurance of the same sufferings we suffer. And our hope for you is firm, because we know that just as you share in our sufferings, so also you share in our comfort.

2 CORINTHIANS 1:3–7

Hebrews again breaks the pattern and lacks a greeting.

4. Next, the author embarks upon the body of the letter.

In this main section of the letter, the author may simply begin by jumping right into the reason, or occasion, for writing the letter. This is what Paul does in Galatians:

I am astonished that you are so quickly deserting the one who called you.

GALATIANS 1:6

However, in many letters there is thanksgiving, such as 1 Corinthians 1:4–9, or a beautiful first chapter such as in Ephesians about being chosen and blessed by the Lord.

5. Then, the author applies his teaching.

Here, the author gives practical guidance to his readers about how to live in light of the teaching. We have one of the best examples of this in James's epistle, where he tells his audience that faith without works is dead faith (chapters 1–2) and then goes on to instruct his readers in some very specific ways to test their faith by their actions (chapters 3–5).

6. Lastly, the author gives his closing greetings.

In an epistle's conclusion, we can find exhortations, a benediction, or a list of people the author wants to point out for their special contribution to the ministry. At the end of Romans, for example, Paul lists over twenty-five individuals and the roles they played in his ministry (Rom. 16:1–16).

WHEN WERE THE EPISTLES WRITTEN?

The New Testament letters appear as early as the late AD 40s, about two decades after Jesus, and span to the twilight of the first century. A critical mass of the letters appears in the AD 60s, including many of Paul's letters, Peter's two letters, and possibly Hebrews. The New Testament letters are our earliest witnesses to the movement of the gospel in the early church.

The epistles are dated by historical markers found in them: names, places, and information about the authors. Sometimes we can corroborate things said in epistles with the narrative in the book of Acts, such as is the case with Paul's travels and imprisonments. For example, we can track down Priscilla and Aquila, who are mentioned in Paul's epistles, in the story in Acts 18 (Rom. 16:3; 2 Tim. 4:19; 1 Cor. 16:19).

The names and places mentioned in the epistles can give us a window into the history behind the letters. This reminds us that Christianity is a historical faith and can be confirmed by many witnesses who lived out their faith and ministered in the church much as Christians do today.

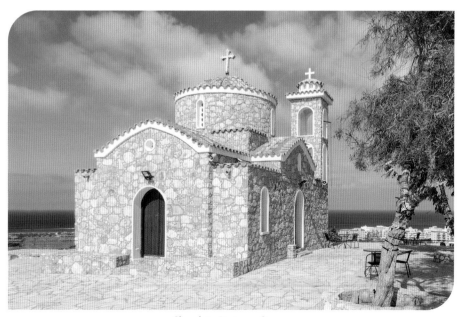

Church in Protaras, Cyprus

BOOK	AUTHOR	DATE	AUDIENCE
ROMANS	Paul	AD 57	Church in Rome
1 CORINTHIANS	Paul	AD 55–56	Church in Corinth
2 CORINTHIANS	Paul	AD 56	Church in Corinth
GALATIANS	Paul	AD 49	Churches in Galatia
EPHESIANS	Paul	AD 60–62	Church in Ephesus
PHILIPPIANS	Paul	AD 60–62	Church in Philippi
COLOSSIANS	Paul, with Timothy	AD 60–62	Church in Colossae
1 THESSALONIANS	Paul, with Silas and Timothy	AD 50–51	Church in Thessalonica
2 THESSALONIANS	Paul, with Silas and Timothy	AD 50–51	Church in Thessalonica
1 TIMOTHY	Paul	AD 62–66	Timothy
2 TIMOTHY	Paul	AD 66–67	Timothy

Dates shown give an estimated time frame in which the book was written.

DESTINATION	THEMES	NOTABLE
Rome	Universal guilt Justification by faith Godly living	Paul's most theologically packed letter
Corinth	The resurrection Practical Christian living	With Romans, one of Paul's longest letters
Corinth	Suffering New covenant Repentance and judgment	Paul's most personal and emotional letter
Galatia	One gospel Justification by faith Adoption	Possibly Paul's earliest epistle
Ephesus	Adoption New lives in Christ Unity	Similar to Romans in structure and topic, but shorter and more like a summary
Philippi	Partnership Humility Rejoicing	The Philippian church was the first church Paul founded in Europe.
Colossae	Christ's supremacy Alive in Christ A new mindset	Also intended to be read by the nearby church in Laodicea
Thessalonica	Encouragement Resurrection Second coming of Christ	Paul and Silas previously had been forced by a mob to leave Thessalonica.
Thessalonica	Second coming of Christ Diligence	Written about six months after 1 Thessalonians
Ephesus	False teaching Church leadership Godly living	In his epistles, Paul mentions Timothy more than any of his other coworkers.
Ephesus	Faithfulness God's Word	Paul's last epistle

Continued on the next page

BOOK	AUTHOR	DATE	AUDIENCE
TITUS	Paul	AD 64–66	Titus
PHILEMON	Paul, with Timothy	AD 60–62	Philemon
HEBREWS	Unknown	AD 60–69	Possibly Jewish Christians
JAMES	James	AD 49	Jewish Christians living outside of Israel
1 PETER	Peter, with Silas	AD 64	"God's elect, exiles scattered" (v. 1)
2 PETER	Peter	AD 64	"Those who … have received a faith" (v. 1)
1 JOHN	John	AD 85–95	Possibly the same seven churches in Revelation
2 JOHN	John	AD 85–95	"The lady chosen by God and to her children" (v. 1)
3 JOHN	John	AD 85–95	Gaius
JUDE	Jude	AD 60s–80s	"Those who have been called" (v. 1)
REVELATION	John	AD 90s	Seven churches in Asia Minor

DESTINATION	THEMES	NOTABLE
Crete	Church elders Teaching Sound doctrine Good works	Titus and 1 and 2 Timothy are Paul's three Pastoral Epistles.
Colossae	Reconciliation in Christ	Paul's shortest epistle; likely sent along with Colossians
Unknown	Superiority of Christ Perseverance	Written more like a sermon than a letter
Unknown	Faith and works Tests of faith	Possibly the earliest of the epistles
Pontus, Galatia, Cappadocia, Asia Minor, Bithynia	Holiness Suffering	Written to regions all in modern-day Turkey
Possibly Asia Minor	Believers' calling False teachers Christ's return	Written shortly before Peter was martyred in Rome
Possibly Asia Minor	Relationship with God Love Christ's incarnation	Least structured epistle, with many themes blended throughout
Possibly Asia Minor	Love Truth	The "lady" may be a metaphor for "the church."
Possibly Asia Minor	Hospitality Good works	Shortest epistle–and shortest book in the Bible
Unknown	Judgment of false teachers Contending for the faith	Two of Jesus' brothers, James and Jude, wrote epistles.
Ephesus, Smyrna, Pergamum, Thyatira, Sardis, Philadelphia, Laodicea	Victory Hope	John received this revelation while exiled on the island of Patmos.

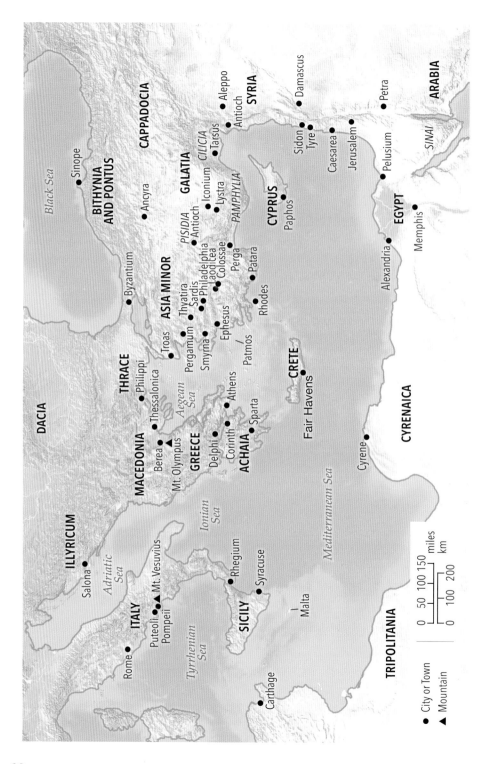

WHAT WAS THE WORLD OF THE EPISTLES LIKE?

The epistles were written and read by people who lived in a setting characterized by three main cultures: Jewish, Greek, and Roman.

Jewish Life

The Jewish life was lived in two general geographic places: the land of Israel and the Diaspora, or dispersion, which was anywhere outside Israel. A Jewish family living in the Diaspora lived among gentiles in pagan cities, which meant an intensely Greek culture. The Diaspora Jews could not live solely Jewish lives, religiously or culturally, since society insisted that they conform to a gentile way of doing commerce, religion, and politics. A Jewish family in the land of Israel was less likely to face the pressure of Greek culture since Jews were the majority. They were free to speak in Hebrew or Aramaic, unlike their Diaspora sisters and brothers who were likely required to speak Greek.

A hard line cannot be drawn between these two contexts since Greek culture did influence the language and thinking in the land of Israel as well, as we can see from some of the Greek translations of the Hebrew Scriptures. Likewise, we notice that some gentiles in the Diaspora converted to Judaism—called God-fearers or proselytes (see, for example, Acts 10:2, 22). This indicates that these two cultures commingled and influenced each other. Though Jews in the first century were far too diverse to boil down to simple characteristics, they still had a clear commitment to the heritage of the patriarchs, the Holy Scriptures, community, family life, and gathering for worship.

Greek Culture

Most of the New Testament Epistles were written to believers who lived in the Diaspora where the culture was largely Greek. This is the "Greco" part of the Greco-Roman world of the first century.

Greek influence, or what we would call Hellenization, can be seen both in language and day-to-day living. Since Alexander the Great in the fourth century BC had dominated the lands from Greece and Egypt to all the way to the current borders of China, the world of the New Testament in the first century AD was thoroughly Hellenized. In each of the lands Alexander conquered, everything from commerce to medicine, literature to religion, philosophy to fashion was influenced by the Greek way of life. Long after Alexander's death, the world remained Greek in culture, even under Roman rule.

Greek became the language of commerce, so by the first century, it took on a basic form called Koine Greek, or "common" Greek. Much like how English is used in many parts of the world today, if you wanted to trade or communicate in New Testament times, you used Greek. The New Testament Epistles were composed in Koine Greek.

The Roman Empire

The world of the New Testament was ruled by the Roman Empire through a system of governors and kings. Rome established their rule over the Mediterranean world by what they called the "Peace of Rome," or *Pax Romana*. Closely tied to Caesar Augustus, the Peace of Rome guaranteed provinces under Roman rule a level of stability and privilege. It also provided citizenship to some people, so long as they did not cause the Roman government any trouble. (Paul's Roman citizenship was especially important to him when it granted him freedom from prison and a direct appeal to Caesar; Acts 16:38; 22:25–27.)

Ara Pacis Augustae in Rome

The Romans carried on the Hellenistic culture of the previous rulers, but they put their own twist on things. They expected a tribute to Caesar to be paid from each province, and, most difficult for early Christians, the Peace of Rome required emperor worship. Originally, the Peace of Rome was based on a cult related to a goddess called *Pax* ("Peace") and her temple *Ara Pacis Augustae* or "Augustan Peace Altar." While other cults existed, the Pax cult was promoted to official status by Emperor Augustus and resulted in full-blown emperor worship. This included public statues of Caesar to remind the provinces of Roman ideals and the divine claims of Caesar. Interestingly, *peace* is often highlighted in Paul's letters with clear association with God, something which would have been understood as a challenge to Caesar's divine rule (Rom. 15:33; 16:20; 1 Cor. 14:33; 2 Cor. 13:11; Phil. 4:9).

WHY DID THE EPISTLES BECOME PART OF THE NEW TESTAMENT?

Even while the New Testament books were being written, the words of people who saw and followed the risen Lord—specifically, the words and writings of the apostles—carried special authoritative weight in the churches (see for example, Acts 1:21–26; 15:6–16:5; 1 Cor. 4–5; 9:1–12; Gal. 1:1–12; 1 Thess. 5:26–27).

> I want you to recall the words spoken in the past by the holy prophets and the command given by our Lord and Savior through your apostles.
>
> 2 PETER 3:2

> But, dear friends, remember what the apostles of our Lord Jesus Christ foretold.
>
> JUDE 1:17

Even well after the apostles' deaths, Christians continued to cherish the testimony of these eyewitnesses and their close associates.

For a writing to be recognized as authoritative in churches throughout the Christian world, the writing had to be connected to an eyewitness of the risen Lord and not to contradict other accepted writings about Jesus. Paul was an eyewitness of the risen Lord and became an apostle (Acts 26:16; 1 Cor. 9:1; 15:8–10). Other epistle writers, such as John, Peter, and James, were present with Jesus during his earthly ministry and became recognized as apostles. Early Christians rejected writings as authoritative that could not meet this criteria. For example, two texts that began circulating among Christians were the *Gospel of Peter* and the *Apocalypse of Peter*. These writings were initially recognized but questioned by church leaders and eventually rejected. They were not accepted because both texts were written in the second century, well after the death of the apostle Peter, and some passages in the *Gospel of Peter* could be seen as suggesting that Jesus was not fully human, a teaching that would contradict other accepted New Testament books.

Although debates continued into the fourth century about a few writings, Christians universally agreed at least as early as the second century about the authority of nineteen New Testament books. Christians unanimously embraced the four Gospels, Acts, Paul's letters, and first epistle of John. Other New Testament books, like some of the General Epistles, became undisputed and officially accepted later in the first few centuries.

Early Lists of Authoritative Christian Writings

FRAGMENT OF MURATORI	CODEX CLAROMONTANUS	EUSEBIUS'S CHURCH HISTORY	LETTER OF ATHANASIUS
Mid 2nd century	Late 3rd century	Early 4th century	AD 367
Apocalypse of Peter was recognized but questioned. Hebrews, James, and the letters of Peter are not mentioned.	*Apocalypse of Peter* and several other texts were recognized but questioned. Hebrews may have been on the list of questioned books.	James, Jude, 2 Peter, 2 and 3 John were recognized but questioned. *Apocalypse of Peter, Gospel of Peter*, and other texts were rejected. Revelation may have been on the list of questioned books.	All 27 books of the New Testament were accepted. No other texts were recognized or accepted.

FRAGMENT OF MURATORI	CODEX CLAROMONTANUS	EUSEBIUS'S CHURCH HISTORY	LETTER OF ATHANASIUS
Accepted Books:	Accepted Books:	Accepted Books:	Accepted Books:
Matthew	Matthew	Matthew	Matthew
Mark	Mark	Mark	Mark
Luke	Luke	Luke	Luke
John	John	John	John
Acts	Acts	Acts	Acts
Romans	Romans	Romans	Romans
1 and 2 Corinthians	1 and 2 Corinthians	1 and 2 Corinthians	1 and 2 Corinthians
Galatians	Galatians	Galatians	Galatians
Ephesians	Ephesians	Ephesians	Ephesians
Philippians	Philippians	Philippians	Philippians
Colossians	Colossians	Colossians	Colossians
1 and 2 Thessalonians	1 and 2 Thessalonians	1 and 2 Thessalonians	1 and 2 Thessalonians
1 and 2 Timothy	1 and 2 Timothy	1 and 2 Timothy	1 and 2 Timothy
Titus	Titus	Titus	Titus
Philemon	Philemon	Philemon	Philemon
1 John	Hebrews	Hebrews	Hebrews
2 or 3 John (or both letters, counted as one)	James	1 Peter	James
Jude	1 and 2 Peter	1 John	1 and 2 Peter
Revelation	1, 2, and 3 John	Revelation	1, 2, and 3 John
	Jude		Jude
	Revelation		Revelation

HOW SHOULD WE STUDY AN EPISTLE?

Much like you would not pick up and read a novel in the same exact way you would a newsletter, we must also approach epistles in a different way than other genres of the Bible. Here are a few tips for how to study an epistle.

1. Identify the genre.

The first step in studying any book of the Bible is to determine what kind of writing it is: a narrative, a book of prophecy or poetry, or in our case, an epistle. It is helpful to also know which type of epistle it is; some epistles were written to a public audience or a church, while others were more private and addressed to an individual.

2. Determine the occasion.

The most crucial step for interpreting an epistle is knowing that it was written for a specific occasion, even when the subject matter is broadly about the faith. In this sense, the epistles are *occasional*. This means that the writers, inspired by the Holy Spirit, wrote to a church, churches, or a person within a specific context with specific concerns, and the letter addresses all these things. Ask yourself, "Why is this letter being written?" This question gets to the heart of the letter's occasion. It may be that the recipients need to be challenged, encouraged, reminded, taught, or corrected—or all the above.

Because the epistles are occasional, this means that when we read these letters two thousand years later, we cannot directly apply what the letter says to our circumstances today without first asking what it meant to those who received the letter. After we ask about the purpose and meaning of the letter to the original audience, then through careful study, we can begin to apply the content of the letter to ourselves and our churches now.

3. Observe the context.

Observing the context could mean asking who the author of the letter is and getting to know more about his credentials, which many writers declare in the first several lines of an epistle. Also, discovering what the author's relationship might be with the recipients can draw out important meaning. For example, some of Paul's letters sound intensely personal, like his correspondence with the Corinthian church or with Timothy, while others have a more distant association, like his letter to the Colossians, which mentions that Paul simply "heard of [their] faith" (Col. 1:4).

Additionally, we might want to find out who the recipients were beyond just the person's name or church location by looking for clues in the letter. For example, Peter wrote his first epistle to Christians who were facing intense persecution, as evidenced when he says, "Dear friends, do not be surprised at the fiery ordeal that has come on you to test you" (1 Peter 4:12) and "After you have suffered a little while, [God] will himself restore you and make you strong" (1 Peter 5:10).

4. Find key themes, words, and structure.

Knowing *what* is in an epistle helps us discover *why* the epistle was written. It can be helpful to identify repeated words or phrases, keeping an eye out for what is emphasized. Readers may also want to outline the epistle's structure to understand the logic and flow of the message. This can be fairly easy to do for a structured epistle like Colossians but more difficult for a free-flowing letter like 3 John.

5. Compare with other epistles.

Readers may want to go a step further and compare key themes and words from one letter to another. For example, some have found parallels between Romans and Ephesians, observing that Ephesians feels very much like a summarized version of Romans. By combining what Paul says about justification in Romans and Ephesians, we may arrive at a more robust theology about this doctrine. Comparing epistles and reading them in harmony can enrich our overall understanding of the message of Scripture.

CHAPTER 2

Paul's Epistles to Churches

ROMANS

Romans is believed to be Paul's "life work," his magnum opus. From creation to Christ, Paul's letter to the Roman church is a densely packed theological narrative whose key emphasis is the gospel as "the power of God" for salvation (Rom. 1:16). Chapters 1–11 lay out Paul's theology and chapters 12–16 apply that theology to godly living.

Who wrote Romans?

Paul claims authorship in the first verse, although Tertius served as his secretary and wrote down the letter (Rom. 16:22). Paul's authorship of Romans has rarely been challenged in scholarship.

When was Romans written?

Though Romans is first among the New Testament epistles, it is actually one of Paul's later epistles,

Etching by Jan Luyken of Paul dictating to Tertius his letter to the Romans

being written during his third missionary journey around AD 57. Bible scholars point to circumstantial evidence that suggests this epistle was written from Corinth, including early manuscript evidence that has the name Erastus as the Corinth "director of public works" (Rom. 16:23). The commendation of Phoebe in Romans 16:1–2, who lived near Corinth, may indicate that she carried the letter to Rome.

Who were the Romans?

Situated in west-central Italy where it still stands today, Rome was the heart of the Roman Empire's culture, governance, and power. Imagine modern-day New York City combined with Washington DC—that was Rome. In Rome, archaeologists have found impressive stadiums, such as the Circus Maximus, as well as theaters and marketplaces, known as forums. These centers of cultural life included many temples to pagan gods, but none of these outshone the devotion to the emperor of Rome. The early emperors had their images throughout the city, all aimed at reinforcing the citizenry's devotion to Caesar. The most notable is the Altar of Peace, representing Peace of Rome, or *Pax Romana*, which undergirded Rome's hold on the known world.

Christianity reached Rome within the first generation of the church and was the farthest northern and western outpost of the church. This is why it was from Rome that Paul hoped to reach even farther to Spain (Rom. 15:24).

Why did Paul write to the church in Rome?

Like many large cities, the population of Rome was diverse in its religious and cultural makeup. This diversity was brought into the church, which was a good thing, but in the earliest days of the church, Jewish and gentile diversity also caused conflict about how to live the Christian life. We can discern from Paul's letter that there was debate over true faith and its origin, as well how the Old Testament law applied to gentiles and Jews.

What is Paul's message to the Romans?

Universal guilt: Paul aims to show that both Jews and gentiles stand condemned before God and fall short of God's glory (Rom. 1–3).

Justification by faith: Salvation and righteousness are only received by faith. Paul shows this by arguing that the law points to humanity's need

Roman Forum, Rome

for righteousness, which we do not have on our own. Then he observes the central place of faith in salvation and God's call upon his elect into new life in Christ (Rom. 3:21–11:36).

Godly living: Paul explains that once a person is saved by faith, then he or she should grow in godliness and other-centered living. Christians should live self-sacrificially, putting the church, the body of Christ, first (Rom. 12:1–15:13).

Key Verses

> For I am not ashamed of the gospel, because it is the power of God that brings salvation to everyone who believes: first to the Jew, then to the Gentile.
>
> ROMANS 1:16

> For all have sinned and fall short of the glory of God, and all are justified freely by his grace through the redemption that came by Christ Jesus.
>
> ROMANS 3:23–24

> Therefore, I urge you, brothers and sisters, in view of God's mercy, to offer your bodies as a living sacrifice, holy and pleasing to God—this is your true and proper worship.
>
> ROMANS 12:1

Contribution to Scripture

Romans is the prime statement of faith concerning God's plan of salvation for the Jew first and then the gentile. In the Bible, there is no clearer and more detailed case made for the mission to the gentiles and all humanity's need for God's justification and applied righteousness in Jesus Christ alone.

SPIRITUAL GIFTS

Four times in his epistles, Paul gives his readers a list of spiritual gifts. These gifts are empowered by the Holy Spirit and given by God to Christians to enable them to build up the church, the body of Christ. "Now you are the body of Christ, and each one of you is a part of it" (1 Cor. 12:27). "There are different kinds of gifts, but the same Spirit distributes them…. Now to each one the manifestation of the Spirit is given for the common good" (1 Cor. 12:4, 7).

EPHESIANS 4:11	ROMANS 12:6-8
Apostles	Prophesying
Prophets	Serving
Evangelists	Teaching
Pastor-teachers (or pastors and teachers)	Encouraging
	Giving
	Leading
	Showing mercy

1 CORINTHIANS 12:8-10	1 CORINTHIANS 12:28-30
Message of wisdom	Apostles
Message of knowledge	Prophets
Faith	Teachers
Healing	Miracles
Miraculous powers	Healing
Prophecy	Helping
Distinguishing between spirits	Guiding
Speaking in tongues	Speaking in tongues
Interpreting tongues	Interpreting tongues

1 CORINTHIANS

Paul's epistle to the Corinthians includes some of the most definitive statements in the whole Bible on unity, the soul, and the body, and how the resurrection of Jesus Christ makes it possible for a divided and immoral church to become a unified and godly witness to their neighbors. In length, 1 Corinthians ranks with Romans as Paul's longest letters, but in contrast to Romans, this letter is deeply personal for Paul.

Who wrote 1 Corinthians?

Like Romans, Paul's authorship of this letter has rarely been challenged in scholarship. Paul says that the letter is also from Sosthenes (1 Cor. 1:1), possibly the synagogue leader who had been persecuted in Corinth (Acts 18:17).

When was 1 Corinthians written?

Paul wrote the letter around the mid-50s, possibly AD 55–56. Some evidence drawn from the book of Acts suggests that Paul wrote this letter at the twilight of his ministry in Ephesus (1 Cor. 16:5–9).

Who were the Corinthians?

The city of Corinth was in southern Greece on a lofty mountain on the Peloponnesian peninsula. Although several miles from the coast, the

Ruins of the temple of Apollo in Corinth

city gained its power from overseeing two major ports of commerce: the Adriatic port of Lechaion and the Aegean port of Cenchreae.

The Corinth to which Paul wrote was actually the second Corinthian city. The original Greek city of Corinth was leveled in a war with Rome in 146 BC. The new Corinthian city founded in 44 BC—although having marks of Roman culture in its city planning, markets, baths, gymnasiums, and temples for the worship of Caesar—remained Greek in its culture and lifestyle.

In Paul's day, Corinth was known as a very immoral place. Unspeakable things happened in Corinth, but those things were not frowned upon. Instead, they were celebrated and counted as worship in some of the exceptionally large temples in the city. Corinth was home to the Doric-style temples to Athena and Apollo and the famed healing temple to Asklepios. Though it is debated which temple it was, first-century historian, Strabo, speaks of one containing a thousand temple prostitutes. Historians agree that Corinth's port location would have encouraged such loose living, since this was common in many Roman port towns. This sort of living infiltrated the life of the church (see, for example, 1 Cor. 5:1).

Why did Paul write to the church in Corinth?

The Corinthian church was being more influenced by their cultural surroundings than the truth of the gospel. Division, worldly living, self-centeredness, and vain attitudes had driven a wedge between believers in the church and also between Paul and the church. (The division between Paul and the church only seems to deepen after this letter, as seen in 2 Corinthians.)

What is Paul's message to the Corinthians?

The resurrection: Chapter 15 is one of the most robust statements about the resurrection in the entire Bible. Paul ends his letter with the reality of the resurrection because it is by the resurrection that the church can be unified, realizing that their lives then would have future spiritual implications.

Practical Christian living: Paul's aim is to unify the church, and this makes 1 Corinthians one of the most practical of letters in the New Testament: ministry (chapter 3), handling disputes (chapter 6), marriage and singleness (chapter 7), food offerings to idols (chapter 8), men and women (chapter 11), the Lord's Supper (chapter 11), spiritual gifts (chapter 12), and "the most excellent way" of love (chapter 13). Unlike Romans, where life application of theology begins midway through the letter, application weaves throughout 1 Corinthians.

Key Verses

> Do you not know that your bodies are temples of the Holy Spirit, who is in you, whom you have received from God? You are not your own; you were bought at a price. Therefore honor God with your bodies.
>
> 1 CORINTHIANS 6:19–20

> So whether you eat or drink or whatever you do, do it all for the glory of God.
>
> 1 CORINTHIANS 10:31

> And now these three remain: faith, hope and love. But the greatest of these is love.
>
> 1 CORINTHIANS 13:13

> For the perishable must clothe itself with the imperishable, and the mortal with immortality…. Then the saying that is written will come true: "Death has been swallowed up in victory."
>
> 1 CORINTHIANS 15:53–54

Contribution to Scripture

The resurrection is at the heart of this letter. Only by the life-giving power of the resurrection is our practical Christian living made possible or given any meaning. Paul says without it we must simply "eat and drink, for tomorrow we die" (1 Cor. 15:32). Instead, because of Jesus' resurrection, believers can be reconciled to one another, live a life of godliness, and have hope that body and soul will be preserved into eternity.

1 CORINTHIANS 13

The beautiful words about love in 1 Corinthians 13 occur in the context of Paul's teachings about spiritual gifts. God gives spiritual gifts to his people for the benefit of the whole church. Paul shows "the most excellent way" (1 Cor. 12:31); that is, when God's people exercise their spiritual gifts in the context of love, they work the way God intends them.

1 GIFTS WITHOUT LOVE = NOTHING (vv. 1–3)

- Tongues
- Prophecy
- Knowledge
- Faith
- Giving
- Martyrdom

2 DEFINITION OF LOVE (vv. 4–7)

Love is
- Patient
- Kind

Love is not
- Proud
- Rude
- Self-seeking
- Easily angered
- A record keeper of wrongs
- A delighter in evil

Love does
- Rejoice with the truth
- Protect always
- Trust always
- Hope always
- Persevere always

Love does not
- Envy
- Boast

3 LOVE NEVER FAILS (vv. 8–12)

Love is the perfect goal and fulfillment of
- Incomplete knowledge
- Incomplete prophecy
- Growth
- Sight/Recognition

These gifts will end
- Prophecy
- Tongues
- Knowledge

CONCLUSION (v. 13)

Love is the greatest

FAITH   HOPE   **LOVE**

2 CORINTHIANS

Second Corinthians is a highly emotive and personal letter for Paul, unlike any of his other epistles. The reason for this emotional letter was the deep offense Paul had taken to the fact that the Corinthian church, a church he loved dearly, had been lured into following other teachers who questioned the legitimacy of Paul's teaching and his credentials as an apostle. Paul defends both in this letter.

Folio from Papyrus 46, 2 Corinthians 11:33–12:9

Who wrote 2 Corinthians?

While Paul's authorship is largely unchallenged, some scholars have questioned whether he wrote 2 Corinthians 6:14–7:1, because the wording seems unlike his other writings. However, Paul is alluding to many Old Testament passages in this section, which could explain this different style. Paul says that the letter is also from Timothy, "our brother" (2 Cor. 1:1).

When was 2 Corinthians written?

Paul wrote this letter to the church in Corinth not long after 1 Corinthians, possibly AD 56 from Macedonia.

Why did Paul write to the church in Corinth?

Division had grown deeper between Paul and the church. The root of the problem was a group of unnamed opponents of Paul. These individuals had created conflict in the church by questioning Paul's apostolic credentials and the legitimacy of his gospel proclamation.

What is Paul's message to the Corinthians?

Suffering: Paul uses his sufferings at the hands of the false apostles and those who would be guided by Satan to show that he embodies the cross of Christ in his ministry (chapter 11). Such suffering, Paul makes clear, is proof that he is called to be a minister of the gospel.

New covenant: Throughout the letter, Paul defends his calling as a minister of the new covenant. In chapters 3 and 4, Paul compares his unveiled message of the gospel to Moses's veiled face, serving to illustrate the revelation that comes in the righteousness of Jesus as Lord and the fulfillment of the Old Testament prophets who pointed to a future new covenant that is now fulfilled (Jer. 31:31–34; Ezek. 36:26–27).

Repentance and judgment: Paul boldly calls the Corinthian church to repentance, framing godly repentance in joy and salvation (2 Cor. 7:4, 10). The fruit of repentance is seen in generosity and love for one another (2 Cor. 8:1–15; 9:6–15). While Paul ends 1 Corinthians with a powerful statement on Christ's resurrection as the reason for his teaching, Paul concludes 2 Corinthians with a powerful warning about Christ's role as judge as the reason for Paul's bold defense of his ministry (2 Cor. 13:1–10).

FOUR CORINTHIAN LETTERS

Second Corinthians is one of at least four letters that Paul wrote to the Corinthian church. His second and fourth letters are our 1 and 2 Corinthians in the Bible, and his first letter is mentioned in 1 Corinthians 5:9, with the third mentioned in 2 Corinthians 2:3–4. Paul's first and third "lost" letters to the Corinthians have never been found.

Key Verses

But we have this treasure in jars of clay to show that this all-surpassing power is from God and not from us. We are hard pressed on every side, but not crushed; perplexed, but not in despair; persecuted, but not abandoned; struck down, but not destroyed. We always carry around in our body the death of Jesus, so that the life of Jesus may also be revealed in our body.

2 CORINTHIANS 4:7–10

Therefore, if anyone is in Christ, the new creation has come: The old has gone, the new is here!

2 CORINTHIANS 5:17

But he said to me, "My grace is sufficient for you, for my power is made perfect in weakness." Therefore, I will boast all the more gladly about my weaknesses, so that Christ's power may rest on me.

2 CORINTHIANS 12:9

Contribution to Scripture

Second Corinthians is passionately autobiographical. In this letter, we see laid bare the honest, bold, and convinced ministry of Paul as he defends his vocation by the old and new covenants and by God's special call upon him as an apostle. In the end, the message of this letter is, in the midst of suffering, to find strength in God's power and glory.

 # GALATIANS

Since the time of the Reformation in the sixteenth century, especially because of the influence of the great reformer Martin Luther, Galatians has held a special place among Paul's letters because of its strong statements about justification in the sight of God by grace and through faith alone and through Jesus Christ alone.

Who wrote Galatians?

Paul's authorship of Galatians is undisputed in scholarship.

When was Galatians written?

Galatians is perhaps Paul's first epistle, written around AD 49, though some scholars date it later, in the AD 50s. Much of the debate about when the letter was written revolves around the question of which part of Galatia Paul was writing to.

Who were the Galatians?

Paul's relationship with the churches in Galatia was a good one according to what he writes in this letter, but which Galatian churches Paul wrote to is a debated question and remains uncertain.

✠ Were they the churches in northern Galatia, modern-day Turkey, which was made up almost totally of Celtic people, the Gauls? The make-up of this population was tribal, and they stayed to themselves. This would favor a later date of writing.

✠ Was Paul writing to southern Galatian churches, like those in the cities of Antioch, Lystra, Iconium, and Derbe? These churches were in a region that was more like a Roman province with its general diversity, including Jewish synagogues and worship of Caesar. Most scholars are of the mind that Paul was writing to the southern Galatian churches, which he ministered to in his first missionary journey (Acts 13–14). This favors an earlier date of writing.

Why did Paul write to the churches in Galatia?

As we observe right away at the beginning of the letter, the young Galatian churches were being distracted from the true gospel to a different gospel (Gal. 1:6–7). Apparently, there were teachers arriving at each church around the area, saying that the Christians needed to follow the law of Moses to be truly saved, which meant being circumcised. Paul was alarmed because the Galatians were forfeiting their liberty found in the true gospel for a "gospel" that enslaved them to works and would not save them.

What is Paul's message to the Galatians?

One gospel: Paul's argument in this letter is that one gospel (and only one gospel) is sufficient to save both Jews and gentiles; there does not need to be a separate gospel for each.

Antioch of Pisidia

Justification by faith: Undergirding the whole letter is the doctrine of justification by faith in Jesus Christ alone (Gal. 2:16). Paul wanted to make clear that nothing can be added to the righteousness that Jesus gives us by faith (Gal. 2:21).

Adoption into God's family: In Galatians 3:15–4:7, Paul gives one of the clearest and most important interpretations of the Old Testament in support of adoption into God's family through faith in Jesus. (His appeal to adoption and God as Father is also seen in Romans 8.)

Key Verses

> Know that a person is not justified by the works of the law, but by faith in Jesus Christ. So we, too, have put our faith in Christ Jesus that we may be justified by faith in Christ and not by the works of the law, because by the works of the law no one will be justified.
>
> GALATIANS 2:16

> There is neither Jew nor Gentile, neither slave nor free, nor is there male and female, for you are all one in Christ Jesus.
>
> GALATIANS 3:28

> Because you are his sons, God sent the Spirit of his Son into our hearts, the Spirit who calls out "Abba, Father."
>
> GALATIANS 4:6

Contribution to Scripture

All Israel had been awaiting the fulfillment of the Abrahamic covenant in which God promised offspring more numerous than the stars in the sky (Gen. 15:4–5). Paul clarifies in Galatians that all those who place their faith in Jesus alone are adopted into God's family and fulfill God's promises to Abraham.

FRUIT OF THE SPIRIT

One of the most well-known parts of Galatians is near the end of the letter where Paul lists the nine fruit of the Spirit. In Galatians 5:13–25, Paul contrasts the life lived according to the flesh (or sinful nature) with life lived in step with the Holy Spirit. "So I say, walk by the Spirit, and you will not gratify the desires of the flesh" (Gal. 5:16).

ACTS OF THE FLESH GALATIANS 5:19-21	FRUIT OF THE SPIRIT GALATIANS 5:22-23
Sexual immorality	Love
Impurity	Joy
Debauchery	Peace
Idolatry	Forbearance (patience)
Witchcraft	Kindness
Hatred	Goodness
Discord	Faithfulness
Jealousy	Gentleness
Fits of rage	Self-control
Selfish ambition	
Dissensions	
Factions	
Envy	
Drunkenness	
Orgies	

EPHESIANS

It has been said that Ephesians is the Cliff Notes version of Romans. In many ways, Ephesians is structured like Romans: the first half is about the truth of God and the gospel message, while the second half is instruction on daily Christian living.

Who wrote Ephesians?

While Paul's authorship is clearly stated in the first verse and has rarely been challenged, some modern scholars give two reasons for wondering if the letter was written by someone imitating Paul: (1) the author does not seem very familiar with his audience, which would be odd since Paul had a close relationship with the Ephesian church (Eph. 1:15; 3:2; Acts 19), and (2) Ephesians is a different style of writing than many of Paul's other epistles. However, while it is true that Paul spent much time with the Ephesians, the epistle may have been intended for a wider audience: more than one congregation

City of Ephesus, Turkey

in Ephesus, as well as possible Christian congregations in various villages in the large Ephesian jurisdiction. The different writing style could easily be accounted for by Paul's use of a secretary to write the letter.

When was Ephesians written?

Ephesians is one of Paul's Prison Letters, since he mentions his confinement in chapters 3, 4, and 6, which would place the date of writing around AD 60–62 while Paul was in Rome.

Who were the Ephesians?

Much like Corinth, Ephesus enjoyed a place of power and influence in its region and was a cultural hot spot because it was a port city. It was known as a central place of education with famous schools and libraries. Ephesus boasted a large theater that held over twenty thousand people and the famous temple to Artemis (see Acts 19). Like other Roman cities, Ephesus included the worship of Caesar (located in the temple of the Divine Julius) and the goddess of Roma, as well as temples to other Caesars: Trajan, Hadrian, and Domitian. Wealth varied in Ephesus, but the city was home to some of the richest elite of the empire.

Why did Paul write to the church in Ephesus?

This epistle is unique because Paul does not clearly state his reason for writing, but rather he simply and magnificently begins with God's redemptive plan in Christ to adopt the elect out of his overflowing love. The closest thing to an occasion for the letter is how Paul praises the Ephesians' faith and says that he prays for them often (Eph. 1:15–19).

What is Paul's message to the Ephesians?

Adoption: Standing at the center of Paul's statement in the first chapter is one of the greatest doxologies in the Bible on adoption into God's family (Eph. 1:3–14). Paul uses the metaphor of adoption to illustrate believers' secure place in God's family. In Paul's day, a child who was adopted could never legally be abandoned. Likewise, God adopts us in love as children secure in his family.

New lives in Christ: Before knowing Christ, Paul explains in chapter 2, the Ephesians did the work of Satan. But because God is rich in mercy, by grace and through faith in Christ, they were saved by God's work of salvation and have new lives. Since God does this work, no one has the right to boast (Eph. 2:8–9).

Unity: There is unity both in the fact that all were all once under Satan's power and that only God did the work of salvation on believers' behalf. There is unity between Jewish and gentile Christians, and—starting in chapter 4 and through the rest of the letter—unity in the family and the church, which stems from walking in love from Jesus (Eph. 5:1).

Key Verses

For he chose us in him before the creation of the world to be holy and blameless in his sight. In love he predestined us for adoption to sonship through Jesus Christ.

EPHESIANS 1:4–5

For it is by grace you have been saved, through faith—and this is not from yourselves, it is the gift of God—not by works, so that no one can boast.

EPHESIANS 2:8–9

There is one body and one Spirit, just as you were called to one hope when you were called; one Lord, one faith, one baptism; one God and Father of all, who is over all and through all and in all.

EPHESIANS 4:4–6

Contribution to Scripture

This letter soars among the other New Testament epistles, contributing to the overall story of the Bible about what God has done on our behalf and what implications that has for how to treat one another and be unified in all aspects of life. In Ephesians, Paul makes the case that God has planned his church since before the earth was formed and planned that each believer would do good works in Jesus. Since this is true, there should be unity in the church, in marriages, and in families. If we submit to Jesus as our king, we should submit out of love to our sisters and brothers.

THE ARMOR OF GOD

One of Paul's most memorable metaphors is the armor of God in Ephesians 6. Paul explains that it is not a worldly war that believers face but a spiritual one. It is a fight against the devil's schemes and spiritual forces in the heavenly realms. God has outfitted believers with armor and weapons specially designed for this struggle.

EPHESIANS 6:13–18

Therefore put on the full **armor of God**, so that when the day of evil comes, you may be able to stand your ground, and after you have done everything, to stand.

Stand firm then, with the **belt of truth** buckled around your waist,

with the **breastplate of righteousness** in place,

and with your feet fitted with the readiness that comes from the **gospel of peace**.

In addition to all this, take up the **shield of faith**, with which you can extinguish all the flaming arrows of the evil one.

Take the **helmet of salvation**

and the **sword of the Spirit**, which is the word of God.

And **pray in the Spirit** on all occasions with all kinds of prayers and requests.

PHILIPPIANS

No matter how difficult the circumstances, looking to the example of Christ is key to finding contentment in—and even rejoicing in—any situation. In understanding Christ's humility, his followers discover the path to unity in Christian ministry. In this way, they become lights to a watching world. This is the message of Paul's epistle to the Philippians.

Who wrote Philippians?

Paul's authorship has rarely been challenged in scholarship. Paul indicates that the letter is also from his ministry partner, Timothy (Phil. 1:1).

When was Philippians written?

Paul alludes to the possibility that his death may be soon, and he mentions Caesar's household (Phil. 1:13, 20; 4:22). Both suggest a date of writing around AD 60–62, while Paul was in Rome, making Philippians one of his four Prison Epistles.

Who were the Philippians?

The city of Philippi was mainly populated by Roman army veterans in 42 BC. It was known for good agricultural land and tax shelters provided directly by Caesar as an Augustan colony. Like many Roman cities, it contained theaters, baths, markets, and worship of the Roman imperial gods.

Acts 16 gives us a picture of who the Philippian church was to Paul. It was the first church he founded in Europe, and it brought to mind important memories for Paul: the imprisonment he and Silas experienced and their miraculous release from jail (Acts 16:16–26); the conversion of their jailer (Acts 16:27–34); and the conversion of Lydia who opened her home to Paul and his companions (Acts 16:11–15). Paul wrote his letter to the Philippians about a decade after founding the church. No doubt much had transpired in the church in the intervening years.

Why did Paul write to the church in Philippi?

Paul wanted to maintain their friendship and partnership in ministry and to encourage them to continue to grow in Christlikeness (Phil. 1:3–11; 1:18–2:18). Other reasons appear later in the letter: extolling the virtues of Timothy's ministry (2:19–24), updating them on Epaphroditus's health (2:25–30), and exhorting Euodia and Syntyche to reconcile (4:2–3).

What is Paul's message to the Philippians?

Partnership in ministry: At the heart of this letter is Paul's gratitude for the support of the Philippian church and their faithful partnership with him. The tone of gratitude and co-laboring can be found throughout this letter.

Christlike humility: Christ's humility is an example of how to view the priorities of life, conflicts, and daily interactions with one another. Stretching from Paul's initial statements of gratitude to a few miscellaneous instructions for the church or individuals are his lofty sayings about Jesus—the example for all believers.

Rejoicing: The word *rejoice* is used eight times in this short letter. Paul's confinement in Rome while awaiting trial made his exhortations to the Philippians to be content and to rejoice in the Lord especially personal and relevant.

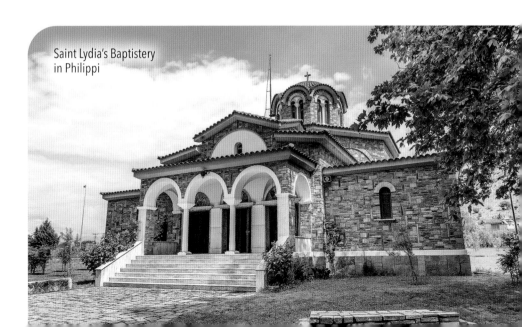

Saint Lydia's Baptistery in Philippi

Key Verses

Being confident of this, that he who began a good work in you will carry it on to completion until the day of Christ Jesus.

PHILIPPIANS 1:6

God exalted him to the highest place and gave him the name that is above every name, that at the name of Jesus every knee should bow, in heaven and on earth and under the earth, and every tongue acknowledge that Jesus Christ is Lord, to the glory of God the Father.

PHILIPPIANS 2:9–11

Rejoice in the Lord always. I will say it again: Rejoice!... Do not be anxious about anything, but in every situation, by prayer and petition, with thanksgiving, present your requests to God. And the peace of God, which transcends all understanding, will guard your hearts and your minds in Christ Jesus.

PHILIPPIANS 4:4, 6–7

Contribution to Scripture

The humility of Christ reverberates throughout this letter. This Christlike humbleness is what leads to greater growth in ministry partnership, unity within the church, and joy in all circumstances, so Christ's followers become light-giving witnesses to the world.

COLOSSIANS

In Colossians, Paul lays out the supremacy of Christ over all things and how, in the process of bringing everything under his rule, believers are also changed into new creations. From this reality, Paul draws specific applications for godly living.

Who wrote Colossians?

Paul wrote Colossians with Timothy (Col. 1:1). Timothy may have been Paul's secretary and did the actual writing of the letter, though Paul signs the letter "in my own hand" (Col. 4:18). The epistle is meant to be read as Paul's teaching since he uses "I" as he instructs the reader, though "we" is used in the opening section for giving thanks for the Colossian church.

When was Colossians written?

This epistle was written when Paul was in prison in Rome around AD 60–62, making it one of Paul's Prison Epistles.

Who were the Colossians?

The city of Colossae was located just east of Ephesus, so this church may have been founded during the time of Paul's ministry in Ephesus, though not directly by Paul himself. Colossae was on the banks of the Lycus River, just a stone's throw from Laodicea and Hierapolis. Little is known about Colossae's history and culture, but its geographical situation places it near many of the earliest Christian congregations in history. Most notably, Colossae is close to the seven churches addressed in John's Revelation.

THE LOST LAODICEAN LETTER

Paul intended his epistle to the Colossians also to be read by the nearby church in Laodicea, and Paul's Laodicean letter (now lost) to be read by the Colossians (Col. 4:16). From this, we can see that it was typical for Paul's letters to be passed around and read to multiple church congregations.

Why did Paul write to the church in Colossae?

The occasion of the letter has puzzled scholars for a long time. Only in Colossians 2 do we get any hint of what the problem might be. Paul warns of "fine-sounding arguments," "hollow and deceptive philosophy," and "human tradition and the elemental spiritual forces" (Col. 2:4, 8, 20–23). Though it is unclear what this specifically refers to, it seems that some type of folk-theology was emerging, possibly related to angels and demons and promoted by soothsayers within the church.

What is Paul's message to the Colossians?

Christ's Supremacy: Chapter one is a stellar explanation of Psalm 110:1, one of the most widely cited Old Testament verses in the New Testament: "Sit at my right hand until I make your enemies a footstool for your feet" (see Matt. 22:44; Acts 2:34–35; Heb. 1:13). Jesus is Lord overall, and because of that, he is reconciling all things to himself.

Alive in Christ: Part of Jesus' reconciling act is to make believers alive in him. This means walking with Christ and being rooted in him (Col. 2:6–7). God makes this possible by first canceling sin and then by triumphing over the world and its rule (Col. 2:13–15).

A new mindset: The resurrection and ascension of Christ lifts one's sight from earthly things to godly things (Col. 3:1–4). Christians must put to death earthly activities and mindsets and, instead set their mind on Christ (Col. 3:5–16).

Key Verses

The Son is the image of the invisible God, the firstborn over all creation. For in him all things were created: things in heaven and on earth, visible and invisible, whether thrones or powers or rulers or authorities; all things have been created through him and for him.

COLOSSIANS 1:15–16

Since, then, you have been raised with Christ, set your hearts on things above, where Christ is, seated at the right hand of God.

COLOSSIANS 3:1

Contribution to Scripture

Colossians is one of the greatest statements in all of Scripture about Christ's position at the right hand of God the Father. Paul describes Jesus Christ as a resurrected and ascended Lord who is using his supremacy and power to reconcile all things and bring believers into new lives of unity and harmony.

1 THESSALONIANS

Paul's first letter to the Thessalonian church is a very encouraging letter, focused on the second coming of Christ as a reason for hope.

Who wrote 1 Thessalonians?

Paul is the author of 1 Thessalonians, along with Silas (Silvanus) and Timothy. Either Silas or Timothy may have been Paul's secretary, but since Paul was not in prison at the time of writing, he may have penned the letter himself without a secretary. Paul uses "we" throughout the letter, as both Timothy and Silas were well known to the Thessalonians (Acts 17:1–10; 1 Thess. 3:6).

When was 1 Thessalonians written?

This is one of Paul's earlier letters, written a few short years after Galatians. If this letter aligns with Acts 18:12–17, which makes mention of Gallio as proconsul of Achaia (AD 51–52), then the letter was written around Gallio's time, during Paul's visit to Corinth.

Who were the Thessalonians?

Historical Thessalonica is located north of Corinth and Athens and west of Philippi. Standing at the Thermaic Gulf of the Aegean Sea, Thessalonica was founded by Macedonian King Kassandros to serve as a port for trade. Direct connection to the Roman Empire is seen by signs of trade by the Via Egnatia and the fact that Mark Antony and Augustus gave the city freedom to govern itself. Even under Roman rule, Thessalonica remained thoroughly Greek in its culture and governance.

Why did Paul write to the church in Thessalonica?

Paul and Silas had been forced to leave the city because of a dangerous mob (Acts 17). Paul spends much of the letter explaining his actions and encouraging the Thessalonian Christians to continue in their diligent faith and love.

Paul also wants to clear up some confusion about the second coming of Christ. The Thessalonian Christians had not yet drawn connections between Jesus' return and their present hope and assurance of resurrection into eternity.

Church of Saint Paul in Thessalonica

What is Paul's message to the Thessalonians?

Encouragement: Paul spends a great deal of the letter recounting his relationship with the church. Unlike some of Paul's other epistles, Paul has nothing but praise for the Thessalonians. They had received the word of God as authoritative and were walking faithfully in brotherly love (1 Thess. 2:13; 4:9–10).

Resurrection and the second coming: The resurrection is the reason those who grieve the loss of loved ones can grieve in hope. The second coming of the Lord will reunite believers with those who have passed away, so believers should encourage one another with this hope (1 Thess. 4:13–18). Jesus' return means believers should soberly take on life's challenges and not skirt responsibilities and expect others to take them on (1 Thess. 5).

Key Verses

Brothers and sisters, we do not want you to be uninformed about those who sleep in death, so that you do not grieve like the rest of mankind, who have no hope. For we believe that Jesus died and rose again, and so we believe that God will bring with Jesus those who have fallen asleep in him.

1 THESSALONIANS 4:13–14

For you know very well that the day of the Lord will come like a thief in the night.

1 THESSALONIANS 5:2

Rejoice always, pray continually, give thanks in all circumstances; for this is God's will for you in Christ Jesus.

1 THESSALONIANS 5:16–18

Contribution to Scripture

First Thessalonians is a perfect example of the "already but not yet" concept. Christians can be presently assured of their salvation (the "already" part) and of the future return of Christ and the resurrection of believers (the "not yet" part).

2 THESSALONIANS

Paul's second letter to the Thessalonian church was written to correct false perceptions of what Paul said in his first letter to them. Apparently, some thought he had said that Jesus was returning so soon that they had missed his second coming. So in 2 Thessalonians, Paul teaches that they should still anticipate Jesus' return and, in the meantime, stand firm in persecution and keep busy doing good.

Who wrote 2 Thessalonians?

As with his first letter, this second letter was authored by Paul along with Silas and Timothy (2 Thess. 1:1). Some scholars in recent times have doubted the authorship of Paul, suggesting that someone else is mimicking Paul's style in the letter. However, since the earliest days of Christianity, Paul's authorship has not been suspect, and Paul even knew that people were trying to mimic him and says so in this letter (2 Thess. 2:2).

When was 2 Thessalonians written?

Paul wrote 2 Thessalonians not long after his first letter to the Thessalonians, AD 50–51, also from Corinth.

Why did Paul write to the church in Thessalonica?

Some false teachers had tried to imitate Paul and Paul's group in their writing and teaching, attempting to persuade the Thessalonians that Jesus had already returned (2 Thess. 2:1–12). Paul exhorts the church to remember his former teachings, to stand firm in the truth, and to pray for him (2 Thess. 2:13–3:5).

What is Paul's message to the Thessalonians?

The second coming: The return of Jesus is a key theme in both Thessalonian letters. In this second letter, Paul explains that (1) the second coming had not yet occurred, (2) Christ's return will be preceded by a rebellion led by Satan and the "man of lawlessness," and (3) the rebellion was at work but had not yet come to a head.

Diligence: Paul's final exhortation is not to simply sit on one's hands and wait for the second coming but to continue to be productive. He warns the Thessalonians to stay away from those who are idle and instead keep busy doing good (2 Thess. 3:6–13).

Key Verses

> Don't let anyone deceive you in any way, for that day [of Christ's return] will not come until the rebellion occurs and the man of lawlessness is revealed, the man doomed to destruction.
>
> 2 THESSALONIANS 2:3

> But we ought always to thank God for you, brothers and sisters loved by the Lord, because God chose you as firstfruits to be saved through the sanctifying work of the Spirit and through belief in the truth.
>
> 2 THESSALONIANS 2:13

> As for you, brothers and sisters, never tire of doing what is good.
>
> 2 THESSALONIANS 3:13

Contribution to Scripture

Paul's second letter to the Thessalonians clarifies what the return of the Lord will look like in contrast to the activity of Satan in the world. Jesus will have ultimate victory, but this does not mean that believers should sit idly waiting. Rather, they are to stay busy in godliness and good works.

CHAPTER 3

Paul's Epistles to Individuals

1 TIMOTHY

This epistle is one of two letters Paul wrote to his young protégé Timothy. In both epistles, we discover practical pastoral advice on dealing with people who want to harm the church, how to lead a church, and specifics on Christian living.

Who wrote 1 Timothy?

Paul's authorship is clearly stated in the first verse, but in recent times some scholars have rejected Paul as the author because of how different this letter and 2 Timothy are from the rest of Paul's epistles. But these differences should be expected since the occasions and purposes differ: 1 and 2 Timothy were written to an individual, not an entire congregation, and contain advice for pastoring rather than exhortation and warnings on more general matters.

When was 1 Timothy written?

Paul wrote his first letter to Timothy in the AD 60s before his final imprisonment in Rome, possibly AD 62–66. As one of his later epistles, this letter is full of Paul's pastoral wisdom, and Paul is beginning to pass the baton to Timothy.

Why did Paul write to Timothy?

Many practical ministry topics are discussed in this letter, but the main

PAUL'S PROTÉGÉ

Timothy was a disciple of Paul, and one for whom Paul had great love (2 Tim. 1:4). Paul knew Timothy's family well, and because of a faithful mother and grandmother, Timothy had grown up in the faith (2 Tim. 1:5). Timothy had traveled extensively with Paul on his missionary journeys, as seen in the book of Acts. He was still a young pastor at this point but one whom Paul trusted to lead with wisdom the church in Ephesus (2 Tim. 2:1–7; 4:1–2).

reason for the letter was a warning about false teachers infiltrating the Ephesian church. Chapter 1:3–20 deals with the false teachers; then Paul returns to the false teachers in two more places: 4:1–5 and 6:3–21.

What is Paul's message to Timothy?

False teaching: No doubt because Timothy was young, others tried to take advantage of him (1 Tim. 4:12). Paul gives Timothy instruction on how to confront the false teachers (1 Tim. 1:3–20), identify false teachers (1 Tim. 4:1–5), and understand their motives (1 Tim. 6:3–5).

Church leadership: If false teaching is a problem, how can Timothy know who the right shepherds and servant-leaders of the church should be? Paul addresses this in chapter three. Just as Paul coaches Timothy on how to identify deceivers, he teaches him how to identify people who will bring health to the church.

Godly living: In three sections of this letter, Paul addresses in detail how a godly life should look: practical Christian living for the general audience and church leaders in 2:1–3:16; for Timothy as their pastor in 4:6–16; and for specific groups in the church in 5:1–6:2.

Key Verses

Command and teach these things. Don't let anyone look down on you because you are young, but set an example for the believers in speech, in conduct, in love, in faith and in purity.

1 TIMOTHY 4:11–12

The elders who direct the affairs of the church well are worthy of double honor, especially those whose work is preaching and teaching.

1 TIMOTHY 5:17

Fight the good fight of the faith. Take hold of the eternal life to which you were called when you made your good confession in the presence of many witnesses.

1 TIMOTHY 6:12

Contribution to Scripture

This first letter to Timothy is one of the most practical guides in Scripture on how to live a godly life, pastor a church, identify those who will aid in the health and growth of a church, as well as watch out for those who seek to harm it.

2 TIMOTHY

Paul's second letter to Timothy is his last words to his young apprentice. In this epistle, we discover the very deep love that Paul has for Timothy and the confidence he has in Timothy's ministry. Along with 2 Corinthians, 2 Timothy is one of the apostle's most emotional letters.

Who wrote 2 Timothy?

Paul wrote this second letter to Timothy. The reasons for accepting Paul's authorship are the same as for 1 Timothy.

When was 2 Timothy written?

This was Paul's last epistle before he was executed, written while he was in prison in Rome, possibly AD 66–67.

PASSING THE BATON OF MINISTRY

In 2 Timothy, we see generations of believers passing the faith on to others: Jesus passes to Paul (1:11), Paul to Timothy (1:13), and Timothy to faithful people who will in turn teach others (2:2).

Why did Paul write to Timothy?

Paul wrote this letter to pass the baton of ministry to Timothy and, through Timothy, to pass the baton to others in the future (2 Tim. 1:1–6). Paul gives Timothy his last mentoring on a life of ministry, which aptly concludes with a strong encouragement to preach God's Word as the heartbeat of his ministry (2 Tim. 4:1–8).

What is Paul's message to Timothy?

Faithfulness: Paul reminds Timothy of his spiritual heritage through his mother and grandmother; and in light of that legacy, Paul encourages him to continue to fan the flame of his gift from God, follow sound teaching, and be unashamed of the gospel (2 Tim. 1:5–14).

God's Word: Beginning in 2 Timothy 3:10, Paul reminds Timothy how the inspired Word of God should have a central place in godly living. The heart of Timothy's ministry should be preaching God's Word in every season and circumstance (2 Tim. 4:1–8).

Key Verses

All Scripture is God-breathed and is useful for teaching, rebuking, correcting and training in righteousness, so that the servant of God may be thoroughly equipped for every good work.

2 TIMOTHY 3:16–17

Preach the word; be prepared in season and out of season.

2 TIMOTHY 4:2

I have fought the good fight, I have finished the race, I have kept the faith. Now there is in store for me the crown of righteousness, which the Lord, the righteous Judge, will award to me on that day—and not only to me, but also to all who have longed for his appearing.

2 TIMOTHY 4:7–8

Contribution to Scripture

After the loss of a major spiritual mentor, many Christians wonder what to do next in their faith. The epistle of 2 Timothy is especially important in this situation. It gives encouraging advice about maintaining one's walk with the Lord and influencing others for the sake of the kingdom of God.

TITUS

Titus rounds out Paul's three Pastoral Epistles. This letter, like both letters to Timothy, hones in on practical Christian living and addresses false teaching within the church.

Titus

Who wrote Titus?

As with 1 and 2 Timothy, Paul's authorship of Titus has been called into question in modern times. However, Paul is clearly stated as the author of this letter (Titus 1:1), and the letter's theology reflects his theology in his other epistles, despite some differences in writing style.

When was Titus written?

This epistle was likely penned between Paul's writing of his two letters to Timothy, around AD 64–66. Paul's location when writing is unknown.

Why did Paul write to Titus?

Like 1 Timothy, false teaching is at the heart of this epistle and provides the occasion for Paul to instruct Titus on how to lead a church with sound teaching and how to appoint of spiritual leaders.

What is Paul's message to Titus?

Church elders: A great number of "rebellious people" and false teachers were seeking to corrupt the churches in Crete, so Paul gives careful instruction to Titus on the qualifications of church elders (Titus 1:5–16).

Teaching sound doctrine: Paul exhorts Titus to be confident and teach the church with authority. Titus's model of godly living is of utmost importance for his congregation (Titus 2:1–15).

Good works: From sound teaching come good works. In chapter 3, Paul says that because of the salvation of Christ and the redemption and washing of the Holy Spirit, believers should submit to church authority, put aside foolish and malicious behavior, and be devoted to good works.

Key Verse

> In everything set them an example by doing what is good. In your teaching show integrity, seriousness and soundness of speech that cannot be condemned, so that those who oppose you may be ashamed because they have nothing bad to say about us.
>
> TITUS 2:7–8

THE GENTILE PASTOR

Titus was a longtime coworker with Paul who became a pastor in Crete (Titus 1:5). He probably converted to Christianity under Paul's ministry, as Paul calls him "my true son in our common faith" (Titus 1:4). Unlike Timothy, Titus was fully Greek (Gal. 2:3). If there was any doubt about Paul's commitment to gentile leadership in the church, Titus puts that doubt to rest. Paul had taught Titus and entrusted him with the authority to appoint church elders in towns across Crete (Titus 1:5).

Saint Titus Basilica in Gortyn, Crete

But when the kindness and love of God our Savior appeared, he saved us, not because of righteous things we had done, but because of his mercy. He saved us through the washing of rebirth and renewal by the Holy Spirit, whom he poured out on us generously through Jesus Christ our Savior, so that, having been justified by his grace, we might become heirs having the hope of eternal life.

TITUS 3:4–7

Contribution to Scripture

Paul's letter to Titus is written with a pastoral heart. The best way to combat false teaching in the church is to model godly living, select qualified and Spirit-led leaders, and teach sound doctrine.

PHILEMON

Paul's epistle to Philemon is his shortest letter and it appears at the end of Paul's thirteen epistles in the New Testament. This brief personal letter was probably sent along with Paul's epistle to the Colossians, both bound for the city of Colossae.

Who wrote Philemon?

Paul is the author of this epistle, along with Timothy (Philem. 1:1). Timothy may have been Paul's secretary for this letter, with Paul the primary author since throughout the epistle the word "I" appears and refers to Paul.

When was Philemon written?

This is one of Paul's Prison Epistles, so along with Colossians, Ephesians, and Philippians, it was written between AD 60 and 62—though some scholars date it earlier, in the AD 50s during one of Paul's other imprisonments.

Why did Paul write to Philemon?

One of Philemon's slaves, Onesimus, had left Philemon in Colossae and encountered Paul in Rome (though we are not told how), where he became a fellow believer. Onesimus may have stolen from Philemon when he left (Philem. 1:18–19). This letter is Paul's appeal to Philemon to receive Onesimus back without penalty, "no longer as a slave, but better than a slave, as a dear brother" (Philem. 1:16). Paul regards both Onesimus and Philemon as brothers in Christ and thus calls them to a higher view of how they should relate to one another, despite their very different social standings.

When reading this epistle, it is important to note that the type of slavery in Paul's day was not the same as colonial slavery many centuries later, which we often think of today. While exploitation and abuse of slaves certainly occurred (see 1 Peter 2:18–20), many slaves were too important to mistreat. Slaves could own property, manage large households or businesses, and with enough money they could buy their freedom and even Roman citizenship.

Onesimus

What is Paul's message to Philemon?

Reconciliation in Christ: Though the social and financial levels of Philemon and Onesimus were radically different, the gospel can unite these two men as brothers in Christ. Paul is confident that Onesimus has become a Christ-follower, so this makes Paul, Onesimus, and Philemon partners in the gospel (Philem. 1:17). This changes everything for Paul!

Key Verses

Formerly he was useless to you, but now he has become useful both to you and to me. I am sending him—who is my very heart—back to you.

PHILEMON 1:11–12

Perhaps the reason he was separated from you for a little while was that you might have him back forever—no longer as a slave, but better than a slave, as a dear brother.

PHILEMON 1:15–16

Contribution to Scripture

Philemon shows the lengths which God intends his gospel to reach. The gospel is not for equals in the world's eyes or those who can pay one another back; it is for those who live on completely different social and economic levels. For these people, the apostle Paul says without hesitation, the gospel must reconcile brother to brother.

MORE THAN PHILEMON

Though named after Philemon, this letter was written to more people than just Philemon. It is addressed first to Philemon, but then it is also addressed "to Apphia our sister and Archippus our fellow soldier—and to the church that meets in [their] home" (Philem. 1:1–2). Apphia and Archippus may have been Philemon's wife and son, or they may have been his sister and a leader of the church that met in Philemon's home. Even such a short personal letter from Paul like this one was meant to benefit the whole church—as it has for centuries of New Testament readers ever since.

CHAPTER 4

General Epistles and Revelation

HEBREWS

Toward the latter half of the first century, the church was facing an onslaught of persecution and needed encouragement to persevere. The book of Hebrews is saturated with Old Testament Scripture and promises and shows how Christ fulfills them all, giving believers hope that they can endure their present sufferings.

Who wrote Hebrews and who read it?

The epistle gets its name "Hebrews" from the church tradition that it was written to Jewish Christians, but both the author and recipients are unidentified in the letter. Yet there is still much we can learn about them: the author is familiar with his readers' circumstances (Heb. 10:32–34; 13:18–19); they share common concerns about the imprisonments of colleagues (Heb. 13:3); they both know Timothy (Heb. 13:23); and from the letter's rich and complex references to the Old Testament, we can see they knew their Scriptures well.

> Now faith is confidence in what we hope for and assurance about what we do not see. This is what the ancients were commended for.
>
> Hebrews 11:1–2

When was Hebrews written?

Most scholars believe the epistle was written before the destruction of the Jerusalem temple in AD 70, because the author makes appeals to temple sacrifices as if those sacrifices were still being practiced (Heb. 7–10, 13). The mention of Timothy (Heb. 13:23) also suggests a date earlier than AD 70, sometime in the AD 60s.

Why was Hebrews written?

Persecution is the clearest reason for the writing of this letter. The writer repeatedly encourages his readers to stand strong in Christ and not turn from him (Heb. 2:1–4; 3:7–4:13; 10:19–39). Also, as seen in Paul's Pastoral Epistles written around the same time, false teachers were infiltrating the church (chapter 13).

What is the message of Hebrews?

Superiority of Christ: In the first ten chapters, the writer uses the Old Testament to lay out a case that Jesus is greater than the Mosaic law, Moses himself, the angels, and the sacrificial system. Jesus is the perfect high priest who made the sacrifice once for all (Heb. 10:1–18). In Jesus is found the goal of the Old Testament.

Perseverance: Because of who Jesus is, believers can endure their present sufferings (Heb. 10–12). In fact, according to the "Hall of Faith" in chapter 11 and the "cloud of witness" in Hebrews 12:1, Christians have many examples of persevering through hardship, and they have a cheering squad.

Key Verses

> Day after day every priest stands and performs his religious duties; again and again he offers the same sacrifices, which can never take away sins. But when this priest [Christ] had offered for all time one sacrifice for sins, he sat down at the right hand of God.
>
> HEBREWS 10:11–12

> Therefore, since we are surrounded by such a great cloud of witnesses, let us throw off everything that hinders and the sin that so easily entangles. And let us run with perseverance the race marked out for us, fixing our eyes on Jesus, the pioneer and perfecter of faith.
>
> HEBREWS 12:1–2

Contribution to Scripture

Written more like a sermon than a letter, Hebrews' detailed arguments from the Old Testament as well as its style and structure make it unique among the New Testament books. Most importantly, it lays out the major aspects of the Old Testament all point to Jesus and his ultimate sacrifice for sin.

HALL OF FAITH

HEBREWS 11	THEIR FAITH	OLD TESTAMENT
Abel v. 4	By faith he brought God a better offering than Cain did.	Gen. 4:2–10
Enoch vv. 5–6	By faith he pleased God and was taken to him, bypassing death.	Gen. 5:21–24
Noah v. 7	By faith he built the ark.	Gen. 6:9–22
Abraham and Sarah vv. 8–19	By faith they followed God and believed God's promise of a son, and by faith Abraham obeyed God to offer that son as a sacrifice.	Gen. 12:1–5; 21:1–7; 22:1–19
Isaac v. 20	By faith he blessed his sons' futures.	Gen. 27:1–40
Jacob v. 21	By faith he blessed Joseph's sons.	Gen. 47:31–48:20
Joseph v. 22	By faith he spoke prophetically of the exodus from Egypt.	Gen. 50:24–25
Moses's parents v. 23	By faith they protected Moses as an infant.	Ex. 2:1–10
Moses vv. 24–29	By faith he chose to be with God's people and kept the first Passover.	Ex. 2:11–15; 12:1–30
Rahab v. 31	By faith she kept the Israelite spies safe.	Josh. 2:1–24; 6:16–17, 22–25
Gideon Barak Samson Jephthah David Samuel vv. 32–38	By faith they faced extreme challenges and persecution yet achieved great victories.	Judg. 6:11–8:35 Judg. 4:1–5:15 Judg. 13:1–16:31 Judg. 11:1–12:7 2 Sam. 2:1–4; 5:1–12 1 Sam. 7:3–17

JAMES

The epistle of James was written to Christians to explain that once they put their faith in Jesus, that faith—that alive and true faith—leads to a life of good works.

Who wrote James?

The "James" identified as the author in the first verse is believed to be the brother of Jesus (Matt. 13:55), as evidenced by a long Christian tradition. Although James was not one of the twelve disciples, he quickly became one of the most influential leaders of the church in Jerusalem (Acts 15:13).

When was James written?

This letter is difficult to date, but since we know that James was martyred around

James the Just

AD 62, we at least can set its date earlier than that. Some scholars place the writing of James around the late AD 40s, since the letter does not mention the Jerusalem Council (Acts 15; AD 49), making James the earliest of the New Testament epistles.

Who was James written to?

The letter is addressed "to the twelve tribes scattered among the nations" (James 1:1), suggesting that James is writing to Jewish Christians living outside the land of Israel, though no more specifics are given.

Why was James written?

James's audience seems to be facing social pressures and persecution and struggling with how to understand the relationship between faith and works.

What is the message of James?

Faith and works: The key theme in this epistle is the relationship between faith and works. Those who hear God's Word must also do what it says. Faith is made alive by good works (James 2:14–27).

Tests of faith: Genuine faith is revealed through tests of faith in how believers conduct themselves regarding perseverance, favoritism, speech, humility, quarreling, arrogance, selfishness, suffering, and prayer.

Key Verses

> Do not merely listen to the word, and so deceive yourselves. Do what it says.
>
> JAMES 1:22

> But the wisdom that comes from heaven is first of all pure; then peace-loving, considerate, submissive, full of mercy and good fruit, impartial and sincere.
>
> JAMES 3:17

Contribution to Scripture

What comes next after a person decides to place their faith in Jesus? James's epistle is unique in how it answers this question. He explains what living faith looks like in practical ways. This kind of faith should spark good works that put others first.

JAMES AND THE SERMON ON THE MOUNT

The themes in the epistle of James reveal just how much James listened to his brother Jesus. We can see James echo the teachings of Jesus, especially those from the Sermon on the Mount (Matt. 5–7).

JESUS	JAMES
"Blessed are the poor in spirit" (Matt. 5:3).	"Has not God chosen those who are poor?" (James 2:5).
"Blessed are those who mourn" (Matt. 5:4).	"Grieve, mourn and wail. Change your laughter into mourning" (James 4:9).
"Blessed are the merciful" (Matt. 5:7).	"Judgment without mercy will be shown to anyone who has not been merciful" (James 2:13).
"Blessed are the peacemakers" (Matt. 5:9).	"Peacemakers who sow in peace reap a harvest of righteousness" (James 3:18).
"When people insult you, persecute you . . . rejoice and be glad" (Matt. 5:11–12).	"Consider it pure joy . . . whenever you face trials of many kinds" (James 1:2).
"Do not store up for yourselves treasures on earth, where moths and vermin destroy" (Matt. 6:19).	"Your wealth has rotted, and moths have eaten your clothes" (James 5:2).
"No one can serve two masters" (Matt. 6:24).	"Friendship with the world means enmity against God" (James 4:4).
"Do not worry about tomorrow" (Matt. 6:34).	"You do not even know what will happen tomorrow" (James 4:14).
"Do not judge" (Matt. 7:1).	"Who are you to judge your neighbor?" (James 4:12).
"Your Father in heaven gives good gifts to those who ask him!" (Matt. 7:11).	"Every good and perfect gift is from above" (James 1:17).
"By their fruit you will recognize them" (Matt. 7:16).	"Can a fig tree bear olives, or a grapevine bear figs?" (James 3:12).

1 PETER

This first epistle of Peter encourages Christians facing persecution. Peter urges his readers to look back to the suffering of Christ and to look forward to their hope in the return of Christ.

Who wrote 1 Peter?

Until modern times, the apostle Peter was believed to be the undisputed author. Because 1 Peter is written in very polished Greek and Peter had been a fisherman, some recent scholars have doubted that Peter could write such a letter. But this too quickly dismisses Peter's abilities. (It had been about thirty years since Peter had left his fishing boat to follow Jesus.) It is also possible that Silas served as Peter's secretary for writing this letter and wrote in advanced Greek (1 Peter 5:12).

When was 1 Peter written?

The epistle was written in the mid AD 60s, possibly AD 64 or a few years earlier. The reign of Emperor Nero (AD 54–68) brought about intense persecution of the church, and this aligns with this letter's message about suffering.

Who was 1 Peter written to?

The letter is addressed in the first verse "to God's elect, exiles scattered throughout the provinces of Pontus, Galatia, Cappadocia, Asia and Bithynia." These regions cover a large area in Turkey today.

Why was 1 Peter written?

The primary reason for the letter is to give pastoral encouragement to those facing life-or-death situations because of their faith in Jesus Christ. In each chapter, Peter addresses his recipients with the hope of salvation in Jesus Christ in a world that is evil. He brings his message home in 1 Peter 4:12–5:11 with a pastoral message of perseverance.

What is the message of 1 Peter?

Holiness: Peter wants his readers to understand that it is no mistake that

GENERAL EPISTLES AND REVELATION

the world does not identify with them, nor support their holiness in Jesus Christ. Instead, Peter explains that they are exiles in this world, but they can have hope of an imperishable inheritance from God (1 Peter 1:13–2:12).

Suffering: Believers can glorify God in how they conduct themselves during hardship. In the final chapters of the epistle, Peter addresses family and community life, shepherding the local church, and what it looks like to suffer faithfully. He says for those who suffer to entrust their souls to a faithful Creator (1 Peter 4:19).

Key Verses

> But you are a chosen people, a royal priesthood, a holy nation, God's special possession, that you may declare the praises of him who called you out of darkness into his wonderful light.
>
> 1 PETER 2:9

> But rejoice inasmuch as you participate in the sufferings of Christ, so that you may be overjoyed when his glory is revealed.
>
> 1 PETER 4:13

> Humble yourselves, therefore, under God's mighty hand, that he may lift you up in due time. Cast all your anxiety on him because he cares for you.
>
> 1 PETER 5:6–7

Contribution to Scripture

With this letter—one of only two epistles by Peter—we get insight into the teachings of one of Jesus' closest disciples and, other than Paul, perhaps the most influential leader of the early church. Peter had suffered much for the sake of Christ, and he wrote this letter just a few short years before he would be martyred for his faith. His perspective on holy living and hanging on to hope no matter what the world throws at us has been an encouragement to Christians throughout the ages.

2 PETER

Second Peter is the last correspondence we have from Peter before he was executed for his faith. Although in this letter Peter writes again about living faithfully as God's chosen people during suffering, in 2 Peter, there is more emphasis on false teachers and the second coming of Christ.

Who wrote 2 Peter?

Peter introduces himself as "Simon Peter, a servant and apostle of Jesus Christ" (2 Peter 1:1). The author says that he was at the transfiguration of Jesus, and from the Gospels we know that the three disciples present were Peter, James, and John (2 Peter 1:16–18; Matt. 17:1–13). This second letter by Peter is written in simpler Greek than that of 1 Peter. However, Peter may have used a secretary to write one or both of his letters, which would account for the different styles.

When was 2 Peter written?

It is believed that Peter wrote his second letter not long after his first letter, around AD 64, though some scholars place the date of writing as late as AD 67. Like his first letter, Peter was writing during a time of persecution, possibly writing from Rome awaiting his execution, which occurred around AD 68 (2 Peter 1:14).

Who was 2 Peter written to?

Second Peter is addressed "to those who … have received a faith as precious as ours" (2 Peter 1:1). If 2 Peter is a follow-up letter to 1 Peter, then Peter is writing to Christians in the same regions of Asia Minor that he specifies in his first letter (see 2 Peter 3:1).

Why was 2 Peter written?

Before Peter was martyred, he sought to give his fellow believers encouragement in their calling from God and warnings about false teachers. Peter says that there is no life and hope in these false teachers but only condemnation. Christians should not be impatient but hope and trust in God's timing for the return of Jesus.

What is the message of 2 Peter?

Believers' calling: God has elected his believers, and from this calling springs forth godliness and good fruits (2 Peter 1:5–11). As Christians face difficult circumstances, they need to be firmly rooted in the truth, which is confirmed in the prophetic word of God (2 Peter 1:12–21).

False teachers: Peter gives warnings about false teachers and criteria by which to evaluate them (2 Peter 2:1–22). These teachers are dangerous and should not be trusted, since their way is doomed.

Christ's return: The assurance of the second coming of Jesus is core to Peter's message of encouragement. Because Jesus is returning, Christians should live in holiness and wait patiently on God's timing with confidence in his promises, understanding that God is patient with those who need to repent (2 Peter 3:8–13).

Key Verses

> His divine power has given us everything we need for a godly life through our knowledge of him who called us by his own glory and goodness.
>
> 2 PETER 1:3

> But do not forget this one thing, dear friends: With the Lord a day is like a thousand years, and a thousand years are like a day. The Lord is not slow in keeping his promise, as some understand slowness. Instead he is patient with you, not wanting anyone to perish, but everyone to come to repentance.
>
> 2 PETER 3:8–9

Contribution to Scripture

In 2 Peter, we get a window into why Christians facing persecution can stand up under it, living holy lives and rejecting false teachings. It is the Lord's return and hope in his faithfulness to his promises that believers look to for confidence that one day they "will receive a rich welcome into the eternal kingdom of our Lord and Savior Jesus Christ" (2 Peter 1:11).

1 JOHN

While the theme of love appears in all three of John's epistles, it thoroughly saturates his first letter. Because of God's love, believers are called to love one another—not only in word but also in deed.

Who wrote 1 John?

Unlike many other epistles, the author of 1 John does not identify himself in the opening. From the earliest days of Christianity, John the son of Zebedee, the beloved disciple, was widely said to be the writer of all three epistles named after him. The most compelling argument for John's authorship is that the style and vocabulary of the three letters are remarkably like the gospel of John.

When was 1 John written?

The three letters of John are among some of the latest epistles of the New Testament. It is believed that John wrote his epistles late in life, possibly from Ephesus. Though we don't know which of these letters John penned first or exactly what year, scholars estimate they were written around AD 85–95.

The apostle John wrote three letters that reverberate with one message: those who are forgiven and believe in Jesus Christ must walk in truth and love, and resist those who try to bring false teachings into the church.

Who was 1 John written to?

First John does not specify the audience, but from the letter we can glean that John knew his readers well, so they were likely congregations in Asia Minor where John ministered. The recipients may have included the seven churches in Asia Minor addressed in Revelation.

Why was 1 John written?

Multiple times in the letter, John says, "I write to you to you so that …" giving his reasons for the epistle. He writes so that

- ✠ their joy will be complete (1 John 1:4),

- ✠ believers will not sin (1 John 2:1),

- ✠ they will remain strong (1 John 2:12–14), and

- ✠ they will know that they have eternal life (1 John 5:13).

John wants the church to stay grounded in their faith and love, especially as false prophets who denied the core teaching of Christ's humanity were trying to lead some Christians astray (1 John 2:26; 4:1–3).

What is the message of 1 John?

Relationship with God: Believers know God and his love through Christ, have forgiveness of sins, and have God's Spirit and word abiding in them (1 John 1:5–10; 2:13–14, 24–27; 4:6–19).

Love: God's love produces love for one another and good works (1 John 3:11–24; 4:7–21). Belief in Jesus produces love for fellow believers and is proof of being born again and loving and knowing God (1 John 4:7–12).

Christ's incarnation: As false prophets were leading some Christians astray by denying the humanity of Christ, John forcefully states that acknowledging that Jesus came "in the flesh" (1 John 4:2) is a test for knowing whether a teaching is from God's Spirit (1 John 4:1–6; 5:6–8).

Key Verses

If we confess our sins, he is faithful and just and will forgive us our sins and purify us from all unrighteousness.

1 JOHN 1:9

Dear children, let us not love with words or speech but with actions and in truth.

1 JOHN 3:18

> This is how you can recognize the Spirit of God: Every spirit that acknowledges that Jesus Christ has come in the flesh is from God.
>
> 1 JOHN 4:2

> Dear friends, let us love one another, for love comes from God. Everyone who loves has been born of God and knows God.
>
> 1 JOHN 4:7

Contribution to Scripture

For John, the love of God and love for one another are essential for remaining grounded in the faith. John hammers home the need to love, that the origin of love is God, and the importance of being careful of those who would teach otherwise—and that this kind of love relationship is only possible through the incarnate Son of God.

2 JOHN

John's second letter is a mix of encouragement and warnings. In this short letter, he commends Christians for walking in truth and love, and he cautions them about false teachers.

Who wrote 2 John?

The author refers to himself only as "the elder" (2 John 1:1). The writing style and vocabulary of 2 John are so similar to the other writings of John that there is little doubt of John's authorship.

When was 2 John written?

As with 1 and 3 John, this epistle was likely written from Ephesus around AD 85–95.

Who was 2 John written to?

The letter is addressed "to the lady chosen by God and to her children"

(2 John 1:1). This is probably a metaphor for the church, since it seems that John is writing to Christians more broadly and not necessarily to a specific individual. John's other writings depict the church as a bride (Rev. 21:2; 22:17) and he often refers to believers as children (1 John 2:1; 3 John 1:4). As with 1 John, the churches who received this second letter were likely churches in Asia Minor.

Why was 2 John written?

Some itinerate preachers, or "deceivers" as John calls them (2 John 1:7), were coming into Christian homes and teaching that Jesus did not take on a human body but merely appeared to have a bodily existence.

What is the message of 2 John?

Love: At the heart of the church should be love for one another.

Truth: Walking in the truth means not being led astray by false teachers. Those who promote falsehoods, like that Jesus was not fully human, should not be welcomed into Christian homes, for doing so is sharing "in their wicked work" (2 John 1:11).

Key Verses

> I am not writing you a new command but one we have had from the beginning. I ask that we love one another. And this is love: that we walk in obedience to his commands. As you have heard from the beginning, his command is that you walk in love.
>
> 2 JOHN 1:5–6

Contribution to Scripture

Second John shows us that the apostles of the early church, like John, taught that Jesus Christ was both the Son of God and fully human. Yet even in the first century, false teachers tried to infiltrate the church and deny the incarnation of Christ.

In John's view, love and truth go hand in hand, for love is characterized by walking in obedience to God's commands, and those commands are the truth.

3 JOHN

This third letter of John is the shortest epistle in the New Testament. It is a brief, personal letter to a man named Gaius commending him for his faithfulness to truth and love for fellow believers.

Who wrote 3 John?

Like in 2 John, the author identifies himself simply as "the elder" (3 John 1:1), but the letter is so much like the writings of John that John has long been the undisputed author of this epistle.

When was 3 John written?

Just as Philemon was Paul's personal letter sent along with his epistle to the Colossians, 3 John may have been John's personal letter delivered along with one or both of his other two epistles (AD 85–95).

Who was 3 John written to?

While there are several men named Gaius (a common Roman name) mentioned in the New Testament (Acts 19:29; 20:4; Rom. 16:23; 1 Cor. 1:14), it is uncertain whether the Gaius whom John addresses in 3 John was one of these men or, more likely, a different person entirely. From 3 John, we see that Gaius was a well-known and respected leader in the church.

Why was 3 John written?

It appears that there was a power struggle going on in the church. A man named Diotrephes was spreading lies about John and other believers, while Gaius was walking faithfully in the truth. At the end of the letter, John expresses his desire to meet with Gaius face-to-face and talk further.

What is the message of 3 John?

Hospitality: Whereas in John's second letter he expressly says not to welcome and support false teachers, in this third letter he emphasizes the importance of showing hospitality to and working with missionaries of the truth (3 John 1:8).

Good works: As in John's other writings, he makes clear in this epistle that people's actions reveal whether they truly know God or not (3 John 1:11).

Key Verses

> We ought therefore to show hospitality to such people so that we may work together for the truth.
>
> 3 JOHN 1:8

> Dear friend, do not imitate what is evil but what is good. Anyone who does what is good is from God. Anyone who does what is evil has not seen God.
>
> 3 JOHN 1:11

Contribution to Scripture

This short epistle serves as a reminder to believers to remain faithful to the truth, unify the church with love and support for one another, and reject all forms of evil deeds.

JUDE

The epistle of Jude is a forceful exhortation to avoid false doctrine and to disallow false teachers into the church to corrupt it.

Who wrote Jude?

The author is Jude, the brother of James and Jesus who is called "Judas" in Greek in the Gospels (Matt. 13:55; Mark 6:3). From the earliest days of the church, Jude has been accepted as the author.

When was Jude written?

This letter's circumstances bear some similarities to 2 Peter, leading some to believe these epistles were written about the same time in the AD 60s. However, a precise date for Jude is difficult to determine, and other scholars place Jude's writing as late as the AD 80s.

Who was Jude written to?

While the letter is simply addressed "to those who have been called" (Jude 1:1), Jude's extensive use of the Old Testament suggests he was writing to Jewish Christians—though the content of the letter could apply just as well to a gentile audience.

Why was Jude written?

Warnings about false teachings take center stage in this epistle. Jude says at the outset that he "felt compelled to write" to urge his readers to contend for the faith because some false teachers in the church had been using God's grace—his free gift of forgiveness—as a license for immorality (Jude 1:3–4).

What is the message of Jude?

Judgment of false teachers: Jude forcefully urges his readers to persevere and have assurance that the false teachers who spread wickedness will face judgment, just as evildoers in the past had been punished by God.

Contending for the faith: In contrast to false teachings, Jude appeals to his readers to persevere in their faith by remembering the words of the apostles. He concludes his epistle with a statement of the faith (a doxology) about the power and the oneness of God and Jesus.

Key Verses

> But you, dear friends, by building yourselves up in your most holy faith and praying in the Holy Spirit, keep yourselves in God's love as you wait for the mercy of our Lord Jesus Christ to bring you to eternal life.
>
> JUDE 1:20–21

> To him who is able to keep you from stumbling and to present you before his glorious presence without fault and with great joy—to the only God our Savior be glory, majesty, power and authority, through Jesus Christ our Lord, before all ages, now and forevermore! Amen.
>
> JUDE 1:24–25

JUDE'S STRANGE QUOTATIONS

Jude quotes Michael the archangel and Enoch (Jude 1:9, 14–15). Where did he get these unusual quotations? He may have obtained them from oral tradition handed down through the rabbis or, more likely, they are from two books: *The Assumption of Moses* and *The Book of Enoch*. These two books are not part of the either Jewish or the Christian Bible. However, they do help historians understand the period between the Old and New Testaments. Jude's quotation of Michael no longer exists (only fragments of the manuscript of *The Assumption of Moses* remain), but his quotation of Enoch can be found in Enoch 1:9.

Contribution to Scripture

Jude's unique contribution to Scripture is that he uses rich Old Testament imagery (and some noncanonical Jewish writings) to establish a case against false teachers and to give assurance to Christians that they can fight for the faith.

REVELATION

Revelation stands out as one of the most unique books in all of the Bible. Many times in the past and present, it has been used to assess the signs of the end times. However, first and foremost, it is a message to seven churches about faithfulness through hardship and about hope in salvation.

Who wrote Revelation?

Though John is identified as the writer of Revelation in the very first verse, what is written is "the revelation from Jesus Christ" (Rev. 1:1). Revelation and the gospel of John share some common elements, suggesting that the same person wrote both books. But Revelation's Greek writing style is different from John's other writings, leading some scholars to conclude that a different John wrote Revelation. However, the apostle John's authorship has a long tradition in church history, stated as early as the second century by church fathers Justin Martyr, Irenaeus, and others.

When was Revelation written?

Some scholars believe that Revelation 11 predicts the destruction of the Jerusalem temple, indicating that the book was written before AD 70 when the Romans destroyed the temple. But most scholars conclude that Revelation was written in the AD 90s because the cities of the seven churches and the circumstances addressed in Revelation are more relevant to the last decade of the first century when Christians faced persecution under Emperor Domitian.

Who was Revelation written to?

The primary audience is seven churches in cities in Asia Minor: Ephesus,

Smyrna, Pergamum, Thyatira, Sardis, Philadelphia, and Laodicea. The wider audience for the book is all God's people who hear the words of Revelation (Rev. 22:18, 21).

Why was Revelation written?

Like many of the later New Testament epistles, Revelation was written to churches facing both the challenges of persecution and false teaching in the church. The revelation given to John by Jesus is meant to fortify believers against the temptations of going the way of the false teachers or watering down their faith by mixing their religion with worldly attitudes and behaviors.

What is the message of Revelation?

Victory: John's visions include metaphors that serve to assure the church of their salvation from enemies. The Lamb, angels, trumpets, bowls of God's wrath, and the new heaven and new earth all illustrate that God is in control and he has a plan to rescue all of his people.

Hope: The final two chapters in this book are all about the hope believers have in a coming future. One day, each believer will enter the new heaven and new earth, where Christ is the radiant sun, and all believers will worship him perfectly. There will be no more sin or evil, death or weeping. There will be the great new Jerusalem in all its splendor where the Lord reigns forever.

Key Verses

Do not be afraid. I am the First and the Last. I am the Living One; I was dead, and now look, I am alive for ever and ever!

REVELATION 1:17–18

They will wage war against the Lamb, but the Lamb will triumph over them because he is Lord of lords and King of kings—and with him will be his called, chosen and faithful followers.

REVELATION 17:14

Look! God's dwelling place is now among the people, and he will dwell with them. They will be his people, and God himself will be with them and be their God. "He will wipe every tear from their eyes. There will be no more death" or mourning or crying or pain, for the old order of things has passed away.

REVELATION 21:3–4

Contribution to Scripture

In Revelation, the story of God's redemption of his people and the condemnation of evil is told in an apocalyptic style. With vivid and evocative imagery, the message of Revelation is for all Christians facing hardship, giving them hope and assurance of the defeat of Satan, the reign of Christ, and the new heaven and the new earth.

THE APOCALYPSE OF JOHN

Apocalyptic writings in the Bible reveal God's hidden plans through visions, symbols, and images. The word *apocalypse* comes from a Greek word meaning "unveiling" or "uncovering." It is this word in Revelation 1:1 that is translated in most English Bibles as *revelation*. In biblical times, apocalyptic writings often came out of periods of intense suffering and persecution. These writings included not only messages of judgment but also of hope for a coming restoration. The book of Ezekiel, many of Daniel's prophecies, and the book of Revelation are apocalyptic.

CHAPTER 5

Who's Who in the Epistles

Alexander

1 TIM. 1:18–20; 2 TIM. 4:14–15

Paul disciplined this Ephesian metalworker for blasphemy, but Alexander continued to do wrong, significantly harming Paul with strong opposition. Paul warned Timothy, "Be on your guard against him" (2 Tim. 4:15).

Andronicus and Junia

ROM. 16:7

They were Greek-speaking Jews (possibly husband and wife) whom Paul greeted in his letter to the Romans. Followers of Christ even before he was, Paul noted they were "outstanding among the apostles." Their dedicated service led to their imprisonment alongside Paul.

Andronicus and Junia

Antichrist (Man of Lawlessness)

2 THESS. 2:3–12; 1 JOHN 2:18–23; 4:2–3; 2 JOHN 1:7

Also called "the man of lawlessness" and "the man doomed to destruction" by Paul (2 Thess. 2:3), the antichrist will proclaim he is God and persecute God's people before suffering utter destruction when Jesus returns. John referred to the antichrist as well but applied the term to anyone who "denies that Jesus is the Christ" (1 John 2:22).

Apollos

1 COR. 1:12; 3:4–6, 21–23; 4:6; 16:12; TITUS 3:13

Apollos was a learned Jew from Alexandria in Egypt. Aquila and Priscilla met him in Ephesus, where he was preaching about Jesus. Once they filled in the gaps in his knowledge of "the way of God" (Acts 18:26), Apollos went on to be a missionary in the Roman province of Achaia and helped oversee the church Paul had founded in its capital, Corinth (Acts 18:27; 19:1).

A divisive clique developed around Apollos's leadership, which the apostle Paul addresses in 1 Corinthians. Apollos left Corinth for a time, likely to avoid the divisions, but he eventually returned at Paul's urging.

Apphia

PHILEM. 1:2

Paul includes her in the address of the epistle of Philemon: "To Philemon … also to Apphia our sister." She may have been Philemon's wife or sister. Church tradition says she was martyred during the reign of Emperor Nero.

Aquila

See *Priscilla and Aquila.*

Archippus

COL. 4:17; PHILEM. 1:2

He was possibly Philemon's son or a leader in the church that met in Philemon's home in Colossae. Along with Apphia, Paul includes Archippus as a recipient of his letter to Philemon, calling him a "fellow soldier." In his letter to the Colossians, Paul urges Archippus to complete the ministry the Lord had given him.

Aristarchus

COL. 4:10; PHILEM. 1:23–24

One of Paul's traveling companions from Thessalonica, he was seized along with Gaius by the Ephesian mob who rioted in the name of the goddess Artemis (Acts 19:23–41). Aristarchus went with Paul to Macedonia and Troas after the riot, and later he accompanied Paul to Rome. Paul mentions Aristarchus's greetings in his letter to Philemon and also to the Colossians, calling him a "fellow prisoner" (Col. 4:10). According to church tradition, he was martyred in Rome during Nero's persecution.

Aristarchus of Thessalonica

Artemas

TITUS 3:12

At the end of his letter to Titus, Paul reveals that he would send either Artemas or Tychicus to help Titus in his duties as overseer of the churches on Crete. According to church tradition, Artemas later oversaw the church in Lystra.

Barnabas

1 COR. 9:6; GAL. 2:1–14; COL. 4:10

Joseph was the real name of this Levite from the island of Cyprus, but the apostles called him Barnabas, which means "son of encouragement" (Acts 4:36). He was a cousin of Mark (who wrote the gospel of Mark) and a fellow apostle and missionary with Paul (Acts 13–15).

Caesar's Household

PHIL. 4:22

From Rome, Paul sent greetings from "Caesar's household" to the Philippian church. This may indicate that some servants or relatives of Emperor Nero had become Christians.

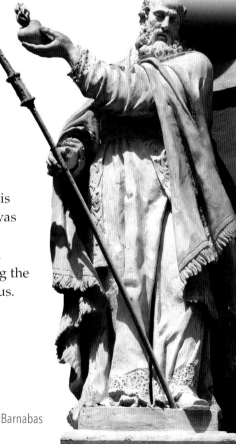

Carpus

2 TIM. 4:13

While traveling through Troas, Paul left his coat and scrolls with Carpus. Later Paul was arrested, hindering his plans to return to Troas. Writing from a Roman prison, Paul asked Timothy to visit him soon and along the way to retrieve his belongings from Carpus.

Cephas

See *Peter.*

Barnabas

Chloe

1 COR. 1:11

While the apostle Paul was in Ephesus, servants or employees of Chloe's household—or of a church that met in her home—told Paul there were divisions in the church in Corinth. Paul penned 1 Corinthians to address these issues and more.

Crispus

1 COR. 1:14

He was the Corinthian synagogue leader who, along with his household, believed in Christ and was baptized by Paul (Acts 18:8).

Demas

COL. 4:14; 2 TIM. 4:9–10; PHILEM. 1:23–24

Paul included Demas's greetings in his letter to the Colossian church and in his letter to Philemon; but later, while Paul was imprisoned in Rome shortly before his death, Demas deserted Paul and went to Thessalonica "because he loved this world" (2 Tim. 4:10).

Demetrius

3 JOHN 1:12

John commended Demetrius as "well spoken of by everyone," indicating that perhaps Demetrius had carried John's third epistle to its recipients.

Diotrephes

3 JOHN 1:9–10

John describes this straying church leader as an unhospitable man who, because he enjoyed putting himself first, had spread harmful gossip about John and his companions.

EMPERORS OF ROME

27 BC–AD 14

Augustus

Also known as Octavian, Augustus was the adopted son of Julius Caesar. After winning control of the empire in the wake of his father's assassination, he was deemed Rome's first official emperor. He was the reigning emperor at the time of Jesus' birth (Luke 2:1).

AD 14–37

Tiberius

Tiberius, a stepson of Augustus, reigned during the ministry of Jesus (Luke 3:1) and appointed Pilate governor of Judea. When Pilate tried to free Jesus, the Jewish leaders claimed Pilate was "no friend of Caesar [Tiberius]" (John 19:12).

AD 37–41

Caligula

Shortly after becoming emperor, illness is suspected as having caused Caligula to become insane, causing him to perform bizarre acts, harming and killing many people. Caligula appointed Herod Agrippa I as king of Judea. After reigning only four years, Caligula was assassinated.

AD 41–54

Claudius

Claudius catered to the Jewish people as a nod to Herod Agrippa's strong support. Yet after Agrippa's death, amid reports of troublemaking, Claudius expelled the Jews from Rome, including Paul's friends Priscilla and Aquila (Acts 18:2).

AD 54–68

Nero

Nero was the Caesar to whom Paul appealed his case, leading to Paul's being sent to Rome (Acts 25:11). He was also the reigning emperor when Peter wrote his first epistle urging Christians to "honor the emperor" (1 Peter 2:17). When a massive fire devastated Rome, Nero blamed the Christians, which lead to a period of intense persecution, during which Peter and Paul were martyred.

AD 68–69

Galba, Otho, and Vitellius

During a period of chaotic civil war, these three emperors held short reigns that ended by murder or suicide.

AD 69–79

Vespasian

Vespasian increased taxation, even laying claim to the temple tax paid by Jews throughout the empire. It was during his reign that Roman forces squashed the First Jewish Revolt, destroying the Jerusalem temple in AD 70. Many Jews were killed or exiled as slaves throughout the empire.

AD 79–81

Titus

Titus essentially co-ruled with his father, Vespasian, during much of his reign, and it was Vespasian who had charged him to lead the army that destroyed Jerusalem in AD 70.

AD 81–96

Domitian

Domitian proclaimed himself to be a god and killed or persecuted close relatives, government officers, and Christians while increasing the army's pay for his own protection. Court officials succeeded in their conspiracy to assassinate Domitian in AD 96. He was the emperor when John was exiled to Patmos where John received visions from God that became the book of Revelation.

Epaphras

COL. 1:7–8; 4:12–13; PHILEM. 1:23

While visiting Paul in Rome, Epaphras reported that false teachers had influenced the believers he served in Colossae, leading Paul to write the book of Colossians. Paul calls Epaphras a "dear fellow servant … a faithful minister of Christ" and his "fellow prisoner in Christ Jesus" (Philem. 1:23).

Epaphroditus

PHIL. 2:25–30; 4:18

Epaphroditus was a gentile member of the church at Philippi, a "brother, co-worker, and fellow soldier" of Paul's (Phil. 2:25). Epaphroditus became sick while traveling to help Paul, who was imprisoned in Rome. He nearly died, but God mercifully healed him, and he returned to Philippi, likely carrying Paul's letter to the church there.

Erastus

ROM. 16:23; 2 TIM. 4:20

This name is mentioned once in Acts 19:22 and twice in the Epistles, each time as an associate of Paul's. It is unknown whether each refers to the

Sosthenes, Apollos, Cephas, Tychicus, Epaphroditus, Caesar, and Onesiphorus of seventy disciples from the Menologion of Basil II

same person. In Romans, Paul describes Erastus as Corinth's "director of public works" (Rom. 16:23). Later, alone in his Roman prison cell, Paul told Timothy that "Erastus stayed in Corinth" (2 Tim. 4:20).

Eunice
2 TIM. 1:5; 3:14–15

Eunice was Timothy's mother, a Jewish Christian who was married to a Greek (Acts 16:1). In his second letter to Timothy, Paul describes both Eunice and her mother, Lois (Timothy's grandmother), as having "sincere faith" (2 Tim. 1:5), and he alludes to one or both of them teaching Timothy the Scriptures "from infancy" (2 Tim. 3:15).

Euodia and Syntyche
PHIL. 4:2–3

Paul urged Philippian church members Euodia and Syntyche to "be of the same mind in the Lord," possibly indicating they had been at odds. He commends them as women who "contended" at his side in "the cause of the gospel."

Gaius
ROM. 16:23; 1 COR. 1:14

Paul passed along Gaius's greetings to the church in Rome, praising him for demonstrating hospitality to him and the entire church at Corinth. This is likely the same Gaius whom Paul baptized in Corinth, along with Crispus, the synagogue leader. He is not, however, identified with the Gaius in Acts 19:29 and 20:4 or the Gaius who received John's third epistle.

Gaius, recipient of 3 John
3 JOHN 1:1–6, 11

The apostle John wrote to Gaius, commending him as a disciple who was walking in the truth and showing hospitality to missionaries. John ends his letter by stating he hoped to share more with Gaius in person.

Gentiles

The ancient biblical prophets stated the promised Messiah would restore wayward Israel and also be "a light for the Gentiles" (Isa. 49:6), referring to people of non-Israelite descent. The New Testament Epistles frequently mention gentiles in the context of their relationship to Jewish people in God's plan of salvation. In Romans, Paul highlights the unity and equality of both people groups, but he also emphasizes that gentile believers should treat Jewish people with respect since Christ, a Jewish man himself, delivered the gospel first to his own people. In the New Testament, the term *Greek* is sometimes used interchangeably with *gentile*.

Hymenaeus

1 TIM. 1:18–20; 2 TIM. 2:16–18

A member of the Ephesian church overseen by Timothy. Hymenaeus, along with Alexander, had abandoned "faith and a good conscience" (1 Tim. 1:19). Paul disciplined them but to no effect. Later, Hymenaeus and a man named Philetus taught falsely about the resurrection of the dead.

James, brother of Jesus

1 COR. 15:7; GAL. 1:19; 2:9–12; JAMES 1:1; JUDE 1:1

This brother of Jesus and Jude was the leader of the church in Jerusalem— or in Paul's words, a "pillar" of the church (Gal. 2:9), and Paul accused them of blasphemy. He is the author of the epistle of James. At the Jerusalem Council, James supported Paul's case for accepting gentiles as members of the church (Acts 15).

James the Just

Jews

The Jews are God's chosen people, descended from the patriarch Abraham, whom God chose to bring the message of Jesus Christ's saving grace to all nations. The New Testament Epistle writers pointed out Jews who embraced the gospel as well as Jews who rejected it and persecuted believers. In Romans and Galatians especially, Paul explains God's plan for the salvation and unity of both Jews and gentiles.

John

GAL. 2:9; 1, 2 AND 3 JOHN; REV. 1:1, 4

John was one of Jesus' first disciples and later became an apostle of the early church. Tradition says he ministered in Asia Minor and was the only apostle not to suffer martyrdom, dying of natural causes in Ephesus near the end of the first century. John is credited with writing a gospel, three epistles that bear his name, and the book of Revelation, a revelation he received while exiled on the island of Patmos.

John the Evangelist

Judaizers

2 COR. 11:1–15, 22; GAL. 2:12–14; 6:13; PHIL. 3:2–3

Judaizers were Christians who mistakenly believed that gentiles must follow Jewish religious laws and customs to be fully made right with God. Often Judaizers would boost their own sense of importance by convincing gentile believers they needed to be circumcised to obtain salvation. Establishing faith alone as a means of justification is a major theme in Paul's writings—largely resulting from the opposition he faced from Judaizers.

Jude, brother of Jesus

JUDE 1:1

Jude, who authored the epistle bearing his name, identifies himself as "a brother of James" (Jude 1:1). He was likely referring to the James who was well known as the Lord's brother and the leader of the Jerusalem church. This would make Jude the brother of Jesus. He is called "Judas" (a Greek variant of his name) in Matthew 13:55 and Mark 6:3.

Junia

See *Andronicus and Junia.*

Linus
2 TIM. 4:21

Paul includes Linus's greeting at the end of his second letter to Timothy. Early church fathers reported that Paul and ordained Linus as overseer of the church in Rome.

Luke
COL. 4:14; 2 TIM. 4:11; PHILEM. 1:24

The author of the gospel of Luke and the book of Acts, Luke was a gentile physician who accompanied Paul on several missionary journeys. In Colossians and Philemon, Paul mentions Luke's personal greetings to the letters' recipients. In 2 Timothy 4:11, Paul notes that "only Luke" was with him while he suffered in a Roman prison cell not long before his death.

Mark (John Mark)
COL. 4:10; 2 TIM. 4:11; PHILEM. 1:24; 1 PETER 5:13

Mark (also called John Mark), author of the gospel of Mark and a cousin of Barnabas, accompanied Paul on his first missionary journey but abruptly left mid-trip (Acts 13:5, 13). This caused a rift between Paul and Barnabas as they were planning their second trip (Acts 15:36–41). Paul was averse to taking Mark again, but Barnabas wanted to give his cousin a second chance. Mark eventually

Mark

regained Paul's trust, becoming one of his most beloved colleagues. In 2 Timothy, written from prison, Paul asks that Mark be brought to him because he is helpful in his ministry. Mark was also a close associate of the apostle Peter, who called him "my son" (1 Peter 5:13). It was likely Peter who furnished Mark with much of the "insider" material for his gospel.

Onesimus

COL. 4:9; PHILEM. 1:8–19

A runaway slave whom Paul led to Christ, Onesimus was a "faithful and dear brother" to many (Col. 4:9). Onesimus had left his master, Philemon, the leader of a house church in Colossae, and met Paul at some point. Apparently Onesimus wanted to be reconciled with his owner, so Paul wrote on his behalf to Philemon, urging Philemon to receive Onesimus as a fellow Christian rather than a slave. Onesimus also served with Tychicus in delivering Paul's epistle to the Colossian church.

Onesiphorus

2 TIM. 1:16–18; 4:19

Paul expressed gratitude for the ways Onesiphorus had helped him while he was in Ephesus and later while he was in chains. When others had abandoned Paul in his Roman prison, Onesiphorus had "searched hard" for Paul (2 Tim. 1:17).

Paul

ROMANS THROUGH PHILEMON; 2 PETER 3:15

Originally known by his Jewish name, Saul, Paul was a Pharisee from the city of Tarsus who persecuted Christians before becoming a Christian himself (Acts 9). Paul preached the gospel throughout the Roman Empire, going on several missionary journeys with various companions and suffering through many imprisonments. Paul performed countless miracles, from healing people's illnesses to bringing the dead back to life, and he was a strong advocate for the inclusion of gentiles in the early church. Paul authored thirteen epistles in the New Testament, sending encouragement and authoritative teaching to various churches and those he had discipled. He is believed to have been beheaded sometime between AD 64 and AD 68, when the Roman emperor Nero was persecuting Christians in earnest.

Peter (Cephas)

1 COR. 1:12; 3:21–23; 9:5; 15:3–5; GAL. 1:18; 2:7–8, 11–14; 1 PETER 1:1; 2 PETER 1:1

Originally named Simon, this impulsive Galilean fisherman became the most outspoken of the twelve apostles. Jesus gave him the nickname Peter, or Cephas in Aramaic, meaning "rock". Following Jesus' resurrection, Peter became a leader, spokesman, and apologist of the early church. His ministry focused on the Jewish people, while the apostle Paul's focused on gentiles. Peter wrote two New Testament Epistles. He is believed to have been martyred in Rome around AD 66–68, during Nero's persecution of Christians. Tradition says he was crucified upside down because he didn't consider himself worthy to die in the same manner as his master.

Philemon

PHILEM. 1:1

From the city of Colossae, Philemon was a coworker of Paul's and hosted a church in his home. Onesimus, a slave of Philemon's, fled for unknown reasons and somehow met Paul. The two formed a bond when Paul shared the gospel and Onesimus believed. Paul wrote to Philemon, asking him to accept Onesimus back as a brother.

Part of a fresco by G. B. Ricci, showing Jesus giving Peter the keys of the kingdom of heaven

Philetus

2 TIM. 2:16–18

Paul warns Timothy about Philetus and Hymenaeus who "departed from the truth," teaching that the resurrection of believers had already taken place.

Phoebe

ROM. 16:1–2

She most likely held an official position of service (deacon/minister) in the church in Cenchreae near Corinth's eastern port. Paul commends Phoebe to the church in Rome, possibly indicating that Phoebe carried Paul's letter from Corinth to Rome. He asked the letter's recipients to receive Phoebe and help her since she had been gracious to many, including Paul.

Paul at the home of Aquila and Priscilla

Priscilla and Aquila

ROM. 16:3; 1 COR. 16:19; 2 TIM. 4:19

These early converts to Christ worked as tentmakers alongside Paul in Corinth and then went with Paul when he started traveling toward Syria. After stopping in Ephesus, Paul continued his journey while Priscilla and Aquila stayed to lead a house church. There they discipled Apollos, who became a prominent leader (Acts 18:1–3; 18–19, 24–26). Paul mentions this couple in his letters to the churches in Rome and Corinth and to his student Timothy, indicating they remained important church leaders. Acts 18:2 states that Aquila was Jewish, so it is likely that Priscilla and Aquila were instrumental in unifying Jews and gentiles in the churches they ministered to.

Rufus

ROM. 16:13

The apostle Paul offered his greetings to Rufus at the end of Romans, calling him "chosen in the Lord" and noting that Rufus's mother had been like a mother to Paul. He may have been the same Rufus whose father, Simon of Cyrene, was forced to carry the cross as Jesus was led away to be crucified (Mark 15:21).

Silas (Silvanus)

2 COR. 1:19; 1 THESS. 1:1;
2 THESS. 1:1; 1 PETER 5:12

Also known by his Latin name, Silvanus, Silas (Aramaic for "Saul") was a leader in the early Jerusalem church (Acts 15:22) and accompanied Paul on his second missionary journey. Silas stayed in Berea with Timothy to serve the new Christians there, while Paul continued his

Paul and Silas are whipped in Philippi

journey to Athens (Acts 17:14). Eventually, Silas rejoined Paul in Corinth, informing Paul of the latest news from Thessalonica (Acts 18:5). Evidently, Silas helped with the writing of both epistles to the Thessalonians, and Silas also assisted Peter with writing his first epistle.

Sosthenes

1 COR. 1:1

Paul describes Sosthenes as "our brother" in the opening greeting of 1 Corinthians. He may have been the same Sosthenes who succeeded Crispus as leader of the Corinthian synagogue (Acts 18:17).

Stephanas

1 COR. 1:16; 16:15–18

Stephanas and his family were the first to become Christians in the Roman province of Achaia. Paul personally baptized them and later commended their devotion and service, encouraging the Corinthian church to look to them as examples of godly leadership. Stephanas, Fortunatus, and Achaicus traveled to visit Paul in Ephesus, likely reporting about divisions in the church at Corinth. They returned carrying Paul's response to their report—the letter of 1 Corinthians.

Syntyche

See *Euodia and Syntyche.*

Tertius

ROM. 16:22

Tertius was Paul's secretary in recording the epistle to the Romans and likely a resident of Rome and known by the church there.

Timothy

ROM. 16:21; 1 COR. 4:17; 16:10; 2 COR.
1:1, 19; PHIL. 1:1; 2:19–23; COL. 1:1;
1 THESS. 1:1; 3:2–6; 2 THESS. 1:1; 1 TIM.
1:2; 2 TIM. 1:2; PHILEM. 1:1; HEB. 13:23

The son of a Greek man and a Jewish believer named Eunice, Timothy was a trusted coworker of Paul's, "my true son in the faith" (1 Tim. 1:2). He delivered many of Paul's epistles, and Paul often referred to Timothy's presence with him or included his name as a coauthor. Paul sometimes indicated he would send Timothy to assist certain churches, such as when divisions erupted in Corinth and when Paul was unable to return to instruct the new Thessalonian believers. Timothy eventually became a pastor in Ephesus, and Paul wrote 1 and 2 Timothy to encourage him in his work there. Hebrews 13:23 mentions that, like Paul, Timothy experienced imprisonment, though we do not know the specific circumstances.

Timothy

Titus

2 COR. 2:13; 7:6–7, 13–15; 8:6, 16–24; 12:18; GAL. 2:1–3; 2 TIM. 4:9–10;
TITUS 1:4

Titus, a missionary and pastor, was one of Paul's most faithful and trusted
companions. Paul sent Titus to Corinth when it was reported there were
divisions within the church. When Paul and Titus reunited, Titus brought
the good news that the Corinthian believers had repented. Titus later
returned to collect an offering for the Christians in Judea. Paul took Titus
with him to preach the gospel on the island of Crete and later wrote the
epistle of Titus to encourage him as he oversaw the church there. Titus
went on a mission to Dalmatia, but according to tradition, he returned to
Crete and served there for many years.

Trophimus

2 TIM. 4:20

A native of Ephesus, he traveled with Paul from Athens to Macedonia and
Troas (Acts 20:1–4) and was with Paul in Jerusalem. Crowds in Jerusalem
rioted because of Paul's teachings and their wrong assumption he had
brought Trophimus, a gentile, into the temple (Acts 21:27–29). In 2 Timothy,
Paul mentions that Trophimus had become ill during one of their previous

Engraving by Gustave Dore of Paul
ending his letter to the Ephesians
before handing it over to Tychicus

journeys, requiring that he stay in Miletus, near Ephesus. According to some church traditions, Trophimus was beheaded by order of the Roman government.

Tychicus
EPH. 6:21–22; COL. 4:7–9; 2 TIM. 4:12; TITUS 3:12

A traveling companion of Paul's and likely a Greek from the city of Ephesus, he accompanied the apostle from Athens to Macedonia and Troas (Acts 20:1–6). Tychicus also acted as a messenger, delivering several of Paul's epistles and providing updates on the well-being of the apostle. Paul described him as an encourager, a dear brother, and a faithful servant in the Lord.

Zenas
TITUS 3:13–14

In his letter to Titus, who was overseeing the churches on the island of Crete, Paul mentions that the church leader Apollos and a lawyer named Zenas would be traveling through Crete. He encouraged Titus to supply them with whatever they needed.

CHAPTER 6

Seven Churches of Revelation

The book of Revelation contains seven letters from Jesus to churches in seven important cities in the Roman province of Asia Minor (modern-day Turkey). In these letters, after a brief but significant description of himself, Jesus addresses the spiritual condition of each church: as appropriate, he praises their strengths, challenges their weaknesses, and symbolically makes a promise to each.

Each letter ends with the similar refrain concerning "the one who is victorious" (Rev. 2:7, 11, 17, 26; 3:5, 12, 21), which points to the main function of the entire book of Revelation: to give assurance and comfort to suffering and persecuted believers. The book assures Christians of the ultimate victory of God and God's people over the powers of evil and death.

> No longer will there be any curse. The throne of God and of the Lamb will be in the city, and his servants will serve him. They will see his face, and his name will be on their foreheads.... And they will reign for ever and ever.
>
> REVELATION 22:3–5

CHURCH	STRENGTHS	WEAKNESSES
EPHESUS Rev. 2:1–7	Perseverance; reject false apostles	Forsaken their first love
SMYRNA Rev. 2:8–11	Endure suffering and poverty, yet are rich	None
PERGAMUM Rev. 2:12–17	Remain true to Christ's name	Tolerate false teachers
THYATIRA Rev. 2:18–29	Deeds, love, faith, and service	Tolerate false prophets
SARDIS Rev. 3:1–6	Some have remained faithful	Deadness
PHILADELPHIA Rev. 3:7–13	Kept Christ's word; not denied his name	None
LAODICEA Rev. 3:14–22	None	Neither hot nor cold; trust in wealth

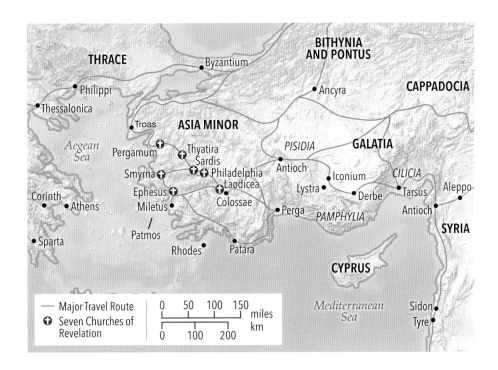

INSTRUCTIONS	PROMISES
Do the things they did at first	Eat from the tree of life
Be faithful to the point of death	Receive life as a victor's crown
Repent	Hidden manna; a new name
Hold on to what they have	Authority; the morning star
Strengthen what remains; wake up	Walk with Jesus; name in the book of life
Hold on to what they have	Kept from the hour of trial; pillar in God's temple
Open the door to Christ; buy riches from Christ	Sit with Christ on God's throne

EPHESUS

Background

✠ An influential commercial and cultural center built in the tenth century BC, the city was the main worship center of the goddess Artemis. Much of the city life and its prestige revolved around the temple and its activities, carried out by thousands of priests and a well-organized temple bureaucracy.

✠ Social, cultural, and legal pressures were probably exerted for all citizens, including Christians, to conform to pagan worship.

Praise

The church in Ephesus is praised for hard work and perseverance, for not tolerating wicked people, for testing the claims of leaders (possibly the Nicolaitans mentioned in Rev. 2:6) and rejecting them when proven false, and for perseverance despite having to endure hardships. The statements build on each other: working hard and persevering translates into not tolerating wicked people and continuing to believe, even though some leaders have tried to negatively influence them. Jesus noted their carefulness and praised it.

Temple of Hadrian, Ephesus

Challenge: Lost First Love

"You have forsaken the love you had at first" (Rev. 2:4). This love probably refers to one of the following:

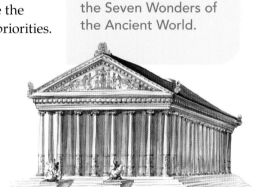

ARTEMIS

Artemis, known in Rome as Diana, was an ancient goddess of hunting and fertility. The Temple of Artemis in Ephesus was one of the Seven Wonders of the Ancient World.

- The burning love for Jesus that believers experience when they first believe, are forgiven, trust in the promise of a new life, and have the desire to put God first in their priorities.

- The love that believers have for one another.

- The love that must always be the moving force for believers.

- The love of witnessing about Jesus to nonbelievers. (Some scholars suggest that because of their focus on rejecting the teachings of false teachers, the Ephesians had given up on testifying about the love of God and salvation through Jesus Christ.)

Regardless of the correct reference, the solution Jesus identifies is clear: "Repent and do the things you did at first" (Rev. 2:5). Love is not an option. It is an integral part of what it means to be part of the body of Christ.

NICOLAITANS

As a group, the Nicolaitans compromised their Christian identity by incorporating pagan practices in their lives. Possibly, they corrupted the teachings of Nicolas from Antioch, one of the church's first deacons (Acts 6:1–5).

SMYRNA

Background

✠ An ancient and wealthy port, Smyrna was one of the most important Roman cities of the area. Emperor worship was central to the life and prestige of the city, although the temple to Athena was also a source of city pride and a significant contributor to the city's economy.

✠ The city had a large population of Jews, many of whom cooperated with the city leaders by persecuting Christians, revealing by their actions that they opposed God ("a synagogue of Satan," Rev. 2:9).

Praise

The Lord praises the church in Smyrna for the richness of their perseverance, faithfulness, and loyalty despite their suffering. "I know your afflictions" is God's reassurance that Jesus knows the afflictions of his people, he cares deeply about them, and he is there with the sufferers (Rev. 2:9). "Yet you are rich" might refer to the following:

FIRST CITY OF ASIA

Ephesus, Smyrna, and Pergamum were the three main cities in the Roman province of Asia. Each one competed with the others to be considered the most important. At different times, both Ephesus and Pergamum served as the capital of the province.

✠ The richness that will come when Jesus returns in glory.

✠ One of the beatitudes: "Blessed are those who are persecuted because of righteousness, for theirs is the kingdom of heaven. Blessed are you when people insult you, persecute you and falsely say all kinds of evil against you because of me. Rejoice and be glad, because great is your reward in heaven" (Matt. 5:10–12).

Challenge: None

"Do not be afraid. … Be faithful" (Rev. 2:10). Smyrna had remained faithful, even in the face of persecution and affliction, and Jesus tells them to persevere because the future holds more suffering. In fact, it is possible that they will have to surrender their lives for the sake of Jesus' name. As tremendous a challenge as this is, however, Jesus is not asking them to do anything he himself was not willing to do.

 # PERGAMUM

Background

⊞ Pergamum was an important center of learning, especially of medicine; the site of the Sanctuary of Asclepius, the god of healing.

⊞ The city contained the second largest library in the ancient world, smaller only than the library of Alexandria in Egypt.

⊞ It was an administrative center for the province; also famous for its emperor worship and its great altar to Zeus.

Temple of Trajan at Acropolis of Pergamum

Praise

Although it struggles in a difficult and demanding society and culture, the church in Pergamum is praised because it retains its loyalty to Christ. In fact, as the death of Antipas suggests, they are willing to die for their faith (Rev. 2:13).

Challenge: Compromise

"Repent therefore!" (Rev. 2:16). Despite their faithfulness, some church members have allowed immoral and wrong teachings to take root in the church. Both Nicolaitans and the followers of Balaam have led some in the church astray, and several now take part in both Christian and pagan practices. The false teachings and practices must be wiped out because evil is insidious and corrosive. However, darkness and lies have no power over light and truth. Lack of repentance will cause judgment: "I will soon come to you and will fight against them with the sword of my mouth" (Rev. 2:16).

BALAAM

In the Old Testament, Balaam was a pagan prophet that Balak, the Moabite king, hired to curse Israel. But God had Balaam speak only what God put in his mouth (Num. 22:35), and Balaam ended up only blessing Israel. Unfortunately, Balaam eventually led Israel to idolatry, and around the time that the New Testament was written, the Jews considered Balaam a prime example of a person whose teachings should not be followed (2 Peter 2:15; Jude 1:11).

PARCHMENT

The word *parchment* is derived from the name *Pergamum*. Although not invented in Pergamum, parchment refers to an animal skin that has been prepared in such a way that it can be written on. It became a common medium for all sorts of documents, including letters and books. Although generally not used today, parchment is still the only material used to make a Jewish Torah scroll.

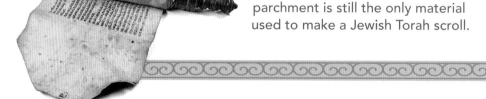

THYATIRA

Background

- ✠ Thyatira was a commercial center, located between Pergamum and Sardis, on an important Roman road.

- ✠ It served as a crucial military post for whoever controlled the area.

- ✠ It was well known for its many trade guilds: craftsmen of wool and linen; makers of leather, bronze, and outer garments; dyers, potters, and bakers; and dealers in slaves.

Praise

The church is noted for its deeds, love, faith, and service and for persevering and constantly improving (Rev. 2:19). The Lord of the universe is aware of what his people are doing and he cares about their actions. Love and faith are the wellspring of the believer's deeds. In other words, our actions, our works, our deeds must be motivated by love and faith. Serving the weak and needy as well as witnessing about the goodness and love of God were characteristic of the church in Thyatira.

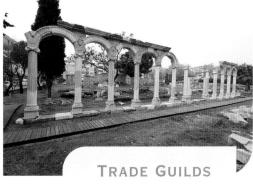

TRADE GUILDS

Trade guilds were associations of artisans who practiced the same craft or sold the same goods. The trade guilds of Thyatira were tightly connected to the pagan religion of the area, so they likely opposed Christianity. Thyatira was the home of Lydia, a dealer of purple cloth and an early Christian believer (Acts 16:14, 40).

Challenge: Tolerating Paganism

"I will repay each of you according to your deeds" (Rev. 2:23). Church members who "tolerate that woman Jezebel, who calls herself a prophet"—in other words, those who allow pagan practices in the church—

will be made to "suffer intensely, unless they repent of her ways" (Rev. 2:20, 22). Church members who have remained faithful to Jesus and his teachings will not have "any other burden" imposed on them, "except to hold on to what you have until I come" (Rev. 2:24–25). Notice that despite their idolatry, Jesus promises a good future if they repent.

JEZEBEL

Jezebel is the name of the wife of King Ahab, king of Israel, in the Old Testament (1 Kings 16:31). She led her husband and Israel to worship the pagan gods of her native land. As used in chapter 2 of Revelation, the name probably refers to an actual person who received the name as an epithet, because of the heretical ideas the individual taught and were accepted by the church.

SARDIS

Background

⊞ Sardis was built high above a plain, making it militarily important, and located on an important highway, making it, at least for a time, a center of commerce; served as the capital of the powerful and wealthy Lydian Empire.

⊞ It was the center for the manufacture of carpets and woolen goods, and also known as the source for nearly pure gold and silver coins and the start of modern currency.

⊞ It was the site of a large synagogue, and a bathhouse-gymnasium complex that covered over five acres.

Praise

It is good that some of the Sardis believers have remained true to the faith; and because they are free of guilt, they will be clothed in white and walk with Jesus and their names will never be erased from the Book of Life (Rev. 3:4–5). But it is bad that in general the Sardis church is stagnant, apparently going through the motions and participating in practices that no longer hold their interest and for which they show little if any enthusiasm. Some believers have actually "soiled their clothes" (Rev. 3:4), a possible reference to the sin of idolatry.

Challenge: The Church Is Dead

The church in Sardis is dead! The diagnosis is a critique on their idolatry, since they might have practiced the cult of Cybele.

This message does not make clear reference to persecution. However, those who are dressed in white and walk with Jesus and are worthy probably refer to those who suffered for the sake of Jesus (Rev. 7:9–17). The challenge to the church in Sardis is to wake up from its spiritual stupor and recall what they had heard and learned.

The message encourages the church in Sardis to remember what they first believed and loved, what they practiced and shared with others. God's people are instructed to remember and act upon that memory and to hold it fast. They must repent of their errant ways.

Today the church also must stand guard against things that, although good, can distract us from God and become idols: money, properties, prestige, education.

The gymnasium complex of Sardis

PHILADELPHIA

Background

✠ Philadelphia was a successful commercial center, mainly because of its being situated at the entrance of a particularly fertile valley, and it was also known for its many temples and religious festivals.

✠ It was prone to earthquakes, because it was located close to an active volcanic region. In AD 17, the city was completely destroyed by a devastating earthquake but eventually rebuilt.

✠ The city was founded only about two hundred years before Christ and named by King Eumenes II for his brother.

Praise

Although very little is known about the church in Philadelphia, it is clear from the letter that in spite of apparently not having a loud voice in the community, it remains faithful and true to Christ. God commends them for having obeyed his "command to endure patiently" (Rev. 3:10). Like all the churches at the time, the church at Philadelphia also experienced persecution.

Ruins of St. Jean Church in Manisa Alasehir, Turkey (ancient Philadelphia)

Challenge: None

"I will . . . keep you from the hour of trial that is going to come on the whole world" (Rev. 3:10). The church in Philadelphia is in very good shape spiritually. Because of their patient endurance and faithfulness, the Lord will spare them from both suffering and being tested by what will come to the world. He encourages them to "hold on to" the strength they have, so they will win the "crown" of eternal life (Rev. 3:11).

Becoming a pillar, a symbol of permanence and stability, is a particular encouragement for believers in Philadelphia because they suffered earthquakes.

God commends endurance, which shows trust in him.

CITY OF BROTHERLY LOVE

Attalus, brother of King Eumenes II, was an accomplished military commander. Because of his loyalty to his brother, he earned the nickname Philadelphus, which means the person who loves his brother. Eumenes even designated that upon his death, Attalus was to be his successor.

LAODICEA

King Eumenes II

Background

✠ This strategic city was located at the crossroads of two crucial trading routes. In Roman times, it was a prosperous commercial center known for its banking, its textile industry (especially its production of black wool), and its school of ophthalmology (noted for an eye salve it developed).

✠ The city was financially strong, even able to rebuild without imperial aid when destroyed by an earthquake in AD 60.

✠ It lacked an adequate water supply, so had an aqueduct built to bring in water.

Praise

This is the only church that does not receive a positive message.

Challenge: Losing Identity in Christ

"I am about to spit you out of my mouth" (Rev. 3:16). In previous messages Jesus' presence brings comfort. Here, however, it is bad news, because the church is "lukewarm," much like the city's water (Rev. 3:16). The church has little, if anything, to offer for spiritual encouragement, refreshment, or growth, because it has lost its focus on Jesus.

The city was located close to a volcanic region. Hierapolis in the north and Colossae in the east had hot and cold waters, respectively. Hierapolis had hot water from its many hot springs, which were considered medicinal.

Ruins in Laodicea

Colossae had cool, refreshing waters that made the entire valley fertile. Their waters were part of their identity as cities. Laodicea, to the contrary, was neither hot nor cold. The accusation seems to say that the church in Laodicea, like the city's water, lacked an identity. Its zeal and love for God had become lukewarm. It had lost its Christian identity!

Preoccupied with acquiring wealth and prestige, the church shows no dependence on God. True riches come only from God, who can clothe them in white and soothe and open their eyes so that they see what is truly important (Rev. 3:18).

"Be earnest and repent" (Rev. 3:19). God's call is to return to faithfulness and perseverance. The church must recognize that it is spiritually bankrupt and has pushed Jesus out of the door! Jesus is there, however, knocking on the door, making his presence available to the church.

JESUS' PRESENCE IN EACH CHURCH

Jesus said to his disciples, "Apart from me you can do nothing" (John 15:5). Our lives, as individuals and in our churches, must reflect our connection to the risen Christ. His example of love, service, humility, sacrifice, and obedience must shape the lives of his followers.

EPHESUS

These are the words of him who holds the seven stars in his right hand and walks among the seven golden lampstands.

REVELATION 2:1

- ✠ The seven lampstands stand for the church in general, and Jesus walking in their midst points to his constant presence with his people.

- ✠ As the lampstands symbolized the presence of God in the tabernacle (Ex. 25:31–37; see also Zech. 4:2–10), they also symbolize the presence of Jesus among his people.

- ✠ The stars could be either heavenly beings or human beings.

- ✠ This description shows that Jesus has authority over the church on earth and in heaven. The final victory of the church depends on the faithfulness of the Lamb and the faithful response of his people, especially in times of persecution and suffering.

SMYRNA

These are the words of him who is the First and the Last, who died and came to life again.

REVELATION 2:8

✠ "The First and the Last" occurs three times in Revelation (1:17; 2:8; 22:13), and it is connected to the self-description of God in Isaiah 41:4; 44:6; 48:12. In Isaiah, the description is used to express that God is the only true God.

✠ This description highlights Christ's divinity and emphasizes that Jesus is the source and the end of all things, he is sovereign over the entire creation, and he is eternal.

✠ Because of Smyrna's political competition with Ephesus and Pergamum to be the most important city of Asia Minor, this description may also be an affirmation that the believers' identity in Smyrna is firmly rooted in a far more stable and legitimate first: Jesus.

PERGAMUM

These are the words of him who has the sharp, double-edged sword.

REVELATION 2:12

✠ Not a military image, this description is further clarified in verse 16 ("the sword of my mouth") and is related to a prophecy about the Servant in Isaiah 49:2 ("He made my mouth like a sharpened sword"); both suggest divine judgment.

✠ Rulings for the entire Roman province of Asia originated in Pergamum, but this image of Jesus shows that he is the true ruler and judge of the church and all of humanity.

THYATIRA

These are the words of the Son of God, whose eyes are like blazing fire and whose feet are like burnished bronze.

REVELATION 2:18

To the one who is victorious and does my will to the end, I will give authority over the nations ... just as I have received authority from my Father.

REVELATION 2:26–27

✠ The "Son of God" reference may have served as a jab at the god Apollo and the emperors who were thought to be sons of the god Zeus.

✠ The description in Revelation 2:18 bears similarities to Daniel's vision of a great man (Dan. 10:4–6).

✠ Psalm 2 describes the nations gathering against the Messiah, the Son of God, yet he rules over the nations as his inheritance.

SARDIS

These are the words of him who holds the seven spirits of God and the seven stars.

REVELATION 3:1

✠ This description refers back to Revelation 1:4, where the seven spirits refer to being empowered by the Holy Spirit. The number seven here does not refer to completeness but to ultimate divine authority. Isaiah 11:2 lists the sevenfold mention of the Spirit.

- The stars refer to the seven messengers who are sent to the churches, carrying the full authority of God to carry out their tasks.

- Jesus, then as now, comes to the church with the fullness of God's authority.

PHILADELPHIA

These are the words of him who is holy and true, who holds the key of David.

REVELATION 3:7

- "Holy" refers to God or to something of God. This description affirms that, unlike the Roman emperors who are false gods, Jesus is the only one worthy of worship and the only one worthy to judge the whole world.

- "True" could also mean "faithful," which is the name of the rider on the white horse (Rev. 19:11). Jesus, who expects faithfulness from the seven churches, is the steadfast one who never changes.

- "The key of David" is an allusion to Isaiah 22:22. Jesus is from the line of David, and just as Jesus holds "the keys of death and Hades" (Rev. 1:18), he also holds the answer for eternal life. Jesus has authority over all creation.

LAODICEA

These are the words of the Amen, the faithful and true witness, the ruler of God's creation.

REVELATION 3:14

✠ This description might refer to Isaiah 65:16, where God's name is mentioned as being used with blessings and oaths. "Amen" probably means "faithfulness" or "trustworthiness." The blessings upon the earth and the swearing of an oath have validity only because they are made effective by God's trustworthiness.

✠ The expression "the faithful and true witness" is similar to the "holy and true" used for Philadelphia (Rev. 3:7). Jesus Christ is "the faithful witness" (Rev. 1:5), because he never changes: "Jesus Christ is the same yesterday and today and forever" (Heb. 13:8).

PERSECUTION AND TRIUMPH

Jesus said, "If they persecuted me, they will persecute you also" (John 15:20). What a puzzling thing to say to his confused and grieving disciples. However, Jesus' point was that God was not abandoning the disciples in their coming sufferings. He promised to be with them, to send the Comforter, the Advocate, the Holy Spirit: "All this I have told you so that you will not fall away" (John 16:1).

As today, the church in the times of the apostles experienced suffering, persecution, and hatred from some people around them. At the end of the first century, at the time when the book of Revelation was likely written, Christians were experiencing different kinds of persecution.

The book of Revelation as a whole was written to give assurance and comfort to suffering and persecuted believers. This theme is crucial in each of the letters to the seven churches. However, each letter assures Christians of the ultimate victory of God and God's people over the powers of evil and death. Jesus' victory over the powers of evil and death is the first decisive step. Christians can claim this victory by being faithful in their devotion to Christ and faithful witnesses of the good news in the world.

CHAPTER 7

Four Views on the Book of Revelation

T he book of Revelation is an exciting yet often misunderstood book of the Bible. Penned in the late first century, it became a source of hope and encouragement for Christians facing persecution.

This chapter compares four different ways Christians throughout the centuries have understood Revelation: the futurist, historicist, idealist, and preterist views. Seeing the different approaches to Revelation will help clarify issues of interpretation and give new insight.

POINTS OF AGREEMENT

Although the book of Revelation allows for many interpretations, all Christians seem to agree that:

- The message of the book is as relevant for Christians today as it was for Christians in the times of the apostles.

- The main purpose of the book is to provide hope and encouragement for believers of all times, especially in times of persecution or suffering.

- The message of the book is clear on at least three points: Christ is coming back and will judge humanity; the powers of evil are doomed before Christ; and God promises a wonderful future for all who believe in Christ.

GOD ACTING IN HISTORY

Both the Old and New Testaments reveal God as Lord over history. Christians of all eras have believed that Jesus will return a second time, but not all Christians have agreed that Revelation is all about the second coming. Whether the visions in Revelation have been, are being, or have yet to be fulfilled is a matter of debate, but the spirit of the last chapter calling on Jesus to come quickly is something all Christians can agree upon—"Come, Lord Jesus!" (Rev. 22:20).

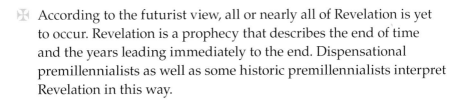

FUTURIST VIEW

✠ Revelation is prophecy primarily about the future end of the world.

✠ Revelation is like a road map for the future.

✠ According to the futurist view, all or nearly all of Revelation is yet to occur. Revelation is a prophecy that describes the end of time and the years leading immediately to the end. Dispensational premillennialists as well as some historic premillennialists interpret Revelation in this way.

HISTORICIST VIEW

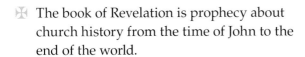

✠ The book of Revelation is prophecy about church history from the time of John to the end of the world.

✠ Revelation is like a history textbook for the past, present, and future.

✠ Historicists view the events in Revelation as symbolic descriptions of historical events throughout church history. Some futurists also understand the seven churches in a historic manner, treating each church as descriptive of a particular era of church history.

IDEALIST VIEW

✠ Revelation is a non-historical and non-prophetic drama about spiritual realities.

✠ It's an allegory for all times and places. The images, visions, and dreams are symbolic expressions of struggles between good and evil throughout time.

✠ This perspective seems to have originated among ancient Alexandrian theologians, who frequently spiritualized and allegorized biblical texts, but this view also has contemporary followers.

PRETERIST VIEW

✠ The book of Revelation is prophecy that was fulfilled primarily in the first century.

✠ Revelation is like an ancient newspaper.

✠ Partial preterists view most of Revelation as prophecy fulfilled in the first century, though the final chapters of Revelation describe future events that will occur at the end of time. Full Preterists contend that the return of Jesus described in Revelation 19 was spiritual and occurred in AD 70. Preterists are typically amillennialists or postmillennialists, though some historic premillennialists might fit in this category.

COMPARING VIEWS ON REVELATION

REVELATION	REVELATION 1:1 "SOON" 1:3 "NEAR" 1:19 "WHAT IS" (See also 22:6, 7, 12, 20)	REVELATION 2:1–3:22 The Seven Churches of Asia Minor	REVELATION 4:1–3 God on His Throne
FUTURIST VIEW	These words refer to the whole of the "last days" or to the quickness with which Jesus will return.	The prophecy begins with the seven churches, which were actual churches in John's day and may also symbolize the types of churches present in the last days.	God gives John a vision from his throne of the events which are to take place "after these things."
HISTORICIST VIEW	The prophecy began to be fulfilled close to the author's lifetime.	The prophecy begins with the seven actual churches in John's day and proceeds through history from there.	God is about to outline his rule over history: the first part of that history is revealed under the vision of the seven seals.
IDEALIST VIEW	Christ is always at hand, near and quick to save his people.	The book begins with the seven churches, which symbolize tendencies in the church that can occur in every age.	God gives John the heavenly viewpoint of the important truths about his power over all things and his care for the church.
PRETERIST VIEW	Near, soon, and quickly are taken literally.	The prophecy begins with the seven actual churches of Asia Minor. It then focuses on the land of Israel before AD 70.	God's courtroom in the heavenly temple is the scene. The Judge on his throne is about to hold court.

	REVELATION 5:1-4 The Scroll	REVELATION 6:1-17 The Seals	REVELATION 7:1-8 The 144,000
FUTURIST VIEW	The scroll could be the title deed to the earth or God's prophetic message in Revelation or God's eternal will and testament.	The seals begin to describe the great tribulation, with each opened seal leading to a greater tragedy upon the earth.	The 144,000 are Jewish Christians in the last days.
HISTORICIST VIEW	The scroll is the coming history of the church as God reveals it and is Lord over it.	The seals are the stages of church history, perhaps describing the church from the late first century AD to the late fourth century.	The 144,000 is a symbolic number that represents the entire church.
IDEALIST VIEW	The scroll is God's will and testament, revealing his salvation plan for all time.	The seals are about recurring evils throughout history and God's authority over them.	The 144,000 are the true spiritual Israel: the church on earth.
PRETERIST VIEW	The scroll is God's bill of divorce against unfaithful Israel, or it is God's eternal will and testament.	The seals describe the Roman war with the Jews which lead to the destruction of Jerusalem (AD 70).	The 144,000 may be the Jewish Christians who escaped the destruction of Jerusalem.

REVELATION 8:1-13 The Trumpets	REVELATION 9:13-19 The Four Angels at the Euphrates	REVELATION 10:8-11 The Little Scroll
The trumpets describe the events of the tribulation in the last days.	The four angels represent the armies of the Orient that will march against Israel in the last days. They will cross the Euphrates as a signal of war.	The little scroll represents the divine plan for the end of the ages, showing that the Word of God is both sweet and bitter to God's prophets and messengers.
The trumpets are the stages of church history, perhaps from about AD 400 until the fifteenth century (or to the present).	The four angels could represent the four principalities of the Turkish empire. The Turks destroyed the last of the Roman empire in AD 1453.	The little scroll may be the Bible at the time of the Reformation. It was sweet to those starved for God's Word, but bitter to those who wanted to control its information and keep it from common people.
The trumpets are about the cycles of human sin, consequences, and God's salvation.	The four angels represent the judgment of God that comes on evil when there is no more restraint, which is represented by the river Euphrates.	The little scroll is the gospel, which must and will be preached to all "peoples, nations, tongues, and kings."
The trumpets represent a vision of the Roman war with the Jews in the first century and extend the seals' description in further detail.	The four angels may represent the four legions of Roman soldiers stationed in Syria that Vespasian led against the Jews (around AD 70). The colors mentioned are Roman military colors.	The little scroll is the same divorce bill as in Revelation 5:1-4 but now unsealed and empty of contents, indicating that the judgments against Israel are now occurring.

REVELATION	REVELATION 11:1-2 The Temple	REVELATION 12:13-17 The Persecuted Woman
FUTURIST VIEW	The measuring of the temple refers to the nation of Israel and the temple that will be rebuilt in the last days. Israel has been restored but still awaits the rebuilding of her faith. This faith will center on the new temple and will eventually lead some Jews to faith in Christ.	The woman is Israel (sun, moon and stars, Gen. 37:9). The child is Christ (rod of iron, Ps. 2:9). The dragon is Satan behind the coming Antichrist. As the head of the revived "Roman Empire," the Antichrist will attack Israel.
HISTORICIST VIEW	The measuring of the temple, the altar, and those who worship there points to God's evaluation of the church, the doctrine of justification by faith, and what constitutes true membership in the church.	The woman is the true church under persecution. The "third of the stars" may refer to the division of the Roman Empire under three emperors in AD 313, or it may refer to post-Reformation divisions in Europe.
IDEALIST VIEW	The measuring of the temple and the leaving of the outer court indicates the division that has always been present between true believers and those who are Christians only in name. The trampling of the court signifies the way the unbelieving world corrupts the church, but this will only be for a short while.	The woman is Israel as the ideal symbol of all the faithful. The child is Christ and the dragon is Satan, the great persecutor of the church in every age. The stars are the angels that fell with Satan at his rebellion. The seven heads and crowns speak of Satan's full political power and authority. The ten horns are military might.
PRETERIST VIEW	The measuring of the temple and its rooms, like the eating of the scroll in chapter 10, mirror what happens in Ezekiel 40–47. Both indicate the destruction of the temple and the separation of the faithful (symbolized by the sanctuary) from the unfaithful (symbolized by the court).	The woman is faithful Israel that gave birth to Christ (the child). The dragon, Satan, persecuted the Messianic church, but she escaped the destruction of Jerusalem by heeding Jesus' words (Luke 21:20–22) and fleeing to the desert hills (the prepared place).

REVELATION 13:18 666	REVELATION 14:14-16 The Son of Man with the Sharp Sickle	REVELATION 15:1-4 The Song of Moses and of the Lamb
It is the number of the future Antichrist– someone who will be like Nero back from the dead.	It is a vision of the coming harvest at the end of the age when Christ will separate the wicked for judgment.	It is the song of salvation from the last-days persecution of the Antichrist and resulting judgment of God. Believers may experience some persecution, but they will not have to endure God's wrath.
It may be the number of the word *Lateinos* and so refers to the Latin or Roman Catholic pope/papacy.	It is a vision of the end of the age when Christ will come and gather his own to himself.	This may be the song of final salvation from the slavery of the abuse of religious and political power among many of the popes.
It is the number of imperfection and human evil that leads to idol worship.	It is a vision of the last judgment and the coming of Christ at the end of the age.	This is the song of salvation that all the redeemed have sung throughout history and will sing anew when Christ comes again.
It is the number that the letters in the name "Nero Caesar" add up to.	It is a vision of the coming of Christ to gather and preserve his church from the judgment that was to befall Jerusalem.	It is the song of salvation from and victory over the ungodly religious and political persecution that Christians suffered in Israel and the Roman world.

	REVELATION 16:10-11 The Fifth Bowl	REVELATION 17:1-18 The Great Prostitute
FUTURIST VIEW	The bowl is the coming judgment upon the revived Roman Empire that will happen in the last days.	The prostitute is the symbol of a false religious system, a new world religious order. The religious coalition will have political influence tied to the power of the Beast (Antichrist) who is the head of the alliance (ten horns) of ten nations in Europe in the last days.
HISTORICIST VIEW	The bowl might be the judgment upon the Roman Pope Pius VI that occurred when the French revolutionary forces stripped the Vatican and took the Pope captive in 1798. The Pope was forced to flee Rome again in 1848. This event was predicted using 1,260 days as 1,260 years (Rev. 12:6).	The prostitute could be the corrupt Roman Catholic Church, including false "Protestant" churches that have come out of her. Her political and religious influence is carried by the beastly Roman papacy and Western European culture.
IDEALIST VIEW	The bowl shows what will happen and does happen to those who steadfastly oppose God. The judgments of darkness and sores recall the plagues of Egypt.	The prostitute is all false and corrupt religion that has allied itself with political power in order to dominate. God warns that such religion shall come to an awful end when true faith triumphs.
PRETERIST VIEW	The bowl is the judgment that fell upon Rome in AD 69. In that single year, Nero committed suicide, three emperors were deposed, civil war set Roman against Roman, and the Temple of Jupiter Capitolinus was burned to the ground, causing darkness during the day.	The prostitute is Jerusalem. Her political and false religious influence is carried by the Roman Empire (Beast). The seven heads are Rome and the first seven emperors, Nero (the sixth of the emperors) ruling at that time. The ten horns are the ten imperial provinces.

REVELATION 18:9-24 The Fall of Babylon	REVELATION 19:1-10 The Marriage of the Lamb and His Bride
The destruction of the coming world religious, political, and economic systems–under the control of the Antichrist and the False Prophet–will be a crash of unparalleled dimension.	The entire church is the bride of Christ whose marriage is announced and celebrated. This scene refers to events near the end of the world and history.
The destruction of Rome (Babylon) will be complete and utterly devastating. The consequences of preaching a false gospel, persecuting true believers, and dabbling in power politics will bring her to this end. Many will mourn her loss, but it will be final.	The entire removal of false religion represented by Rome (Babylon) will leave the faithful to accomplish the purpose for which Christ came–the evangelization of the rest of the world. All people will be invited to come into a relationship (with God the marriage feast with God).
The destruction of Babylon reveals that God's judgment is complete and final. Whether it is Nineveh, Babylon, Rome, or any other economic power that opposes God, it is destined to fail.	Ancient Jewish weddings may be a helpful metaphor. The prophets announced the wedding. Jesus comes and betroths his bride (the church), paying the dowry on the cross. When Jesus comes again, he will offer his bride a wedding feast.
The destruction of Jerusalem (Babylon) is sudden and complete. The misery and the economic disaster is nearly indescribable and a source of great despair. To this day, the temple has never been rebuilt.	The entire book has been about faithfulness using the image of marriage: the divorce bill in chapter 5, the imagery of the persecuted woman, and the prostitute. The book builds toward the marriage feast of Christ and his church.

	REVELATION 20:1-15 The Millennium	REVELATION 21:1-27 The New Creation	REVELATION 22:1-21 The Salvation and Healing of the Nations
FUTURIST VIEW	The millennium is the future physical reign of Jesus Christ on earth.	The new creation will come when Christ comes again and ushers in the age to come.	It will continue until the great tribulation when the Antichrist will temporarily prevail. Christ in his second coming will triumph and usher in the final salvation of the faithful.
HISTORICIST VIEW	The millennium is Christ's present spiritual reign in the lives of his people.	The new creation will come with Christ at his second coming, yet there is a real sense that it has already arrived in the believer's heart. Christians live now as citizens of the New Jerusalem.	It is happening now and will finally be completed when Christ returns.
IDEALIST VIEW	The millennium is Christ's present spiritual reign in the lives of his people.	The new creation is something God continually does with each new day. Yet there will come a day when Christ will personally return and make all things new.	It is what God has always been doing in the world–seeking and saving the lost. Christ will bring all things right when he returns.
PRETERIST VIEW	In partial preterism, the millennium may be Christ's literal reign on earth or a spiritual reign. In full preterism, the millennium is Christ's spiritual return and reign, beginning in the first century.	The new creation is now and future. Since the destruction of the old Jerusalem, Christians have been building the New Jerusalem wherever the gospel is believed, as well as expecting it in full when Christ returns.	It will continue as the gospel grows and spreads throughout the world. Jesus will finalize and renew all things when he comes.

VIEWS OF THE MILLENNIUM

Revelation 20, the only direct reference in the Bible to a reign of Christ that lasts one thousand years, is one of the most controversial sections of the Bible. There are three basic views—premillennialism, amillennialism and postmillennialism—that help to categorize the different interpretations.

- **Premillennialism** holds that Christ will return before the millennium. Jesus will rule the world and begin an age of peace and security. There are two types of premillennialism: historical premillennialism and dispensational premillennialism.

  - *Historical premillennialism* is the belief that Christ will return at the end of the great tribulation. This time of tribulation may last seven years, or "seven" may symbolically refer to the completeness of this tribulation. The church will go through this time of trouble but endure to greet Christ when he comes.

  - *Dispensational premillennialism* is the belief that the church will not endure the great tribulation. Christ will remove the church before that time or at some point before the worst experiences of the tribulation.

- **Amillennialism** is the belief that the millennium is not literally one thousand years but refers to the period now in progress in which the gospel is spreading throughout the world and Christ is ruling at the right hand of God the Father.

- **Postmillennialism** is the belief that there will be a period of great peace and security when the gospel has spread throughout the world and Christ reigns spiritually, through his people. After this time of one thousand years or so, Christ will return to end history.

SEVEN MESSAGES TO CHURCHES
REVELATION 1:1–3:22

Introduction (1:1–8)
Blessing
Vision of Christ

Messages to the Churches

1. EPHESUS
Praise: Hard work, perseverance
Criticism: Forgot first love
Exhortation: Repent
Reward: Authority to eat from the tree of life

2. SMYRNA
Praise: You are rich!
Criticism: None
Exhortation: Be faithful
Reward: Not hurt by second death

3. PERGAMUM
Praise: Remain faithful
Criticism: Idolatry and sexual immorality
Exhortation: Repent
Reward: A white stone with a new name

4. THYATIRA
Praise: Deeds, love and faith, and perseverance
Criticism: Idolatry and sexual immorality
Exhortation: "Hold on to what you have until I come"
Reward: The morning star

5. SARDIS
Praise: None
Criticism: "You are dead"
Exhortation: Wake up
Reward: Be dressed in white, never blotted out from the book of life

6. PHILADELPHIA
Praise: Deeds and faithfulness
Criticism: None
Exhortation: Hold on to what you have
Reward: Become a pillar of the temple

7. LAODICEA
Praise: None
Criticism: You are lukewarm
Exhortation: Be earnest and repent
Reward: Will be seated with Christ

2 SEVEN SEALS
REVELATION 4:1–8:5

Interlude

Vision of Heaven (4:1–11)
Scroll with Seven Seals, and the Lamb (5:1–14)

Opening of Seals (6:1–8:5)

1. **FIRST SEAL**
White Horse — Conqueror

2. **SECOND SEAL**
Red Horse — No peace

3. **THIRD SEAL**
Black Horse — Famine

4. **FOURTH SEAL**
Pale Horse — Pestilence

5. **FIFTH SEAL**
Martyrs under the altar

6. **SIXTH SEAL**
Earthquake, sun black

Interlude

144,000 Sealed (7:1–8)
The Great Multitude (7:9–17)

7. **SEVENTH SEAL**
It contains seven angels with trumpets (8:1–2)
The angel with a golden censer (8:3–5)

3 SEVEN TRUMPETS
REVELATION 8:6–11:19

1. **FIRST TRUMPET**
   Hail, fire, blood; third of earth burned

2. **SECOND TRUMPET**
   Fiery mountain in sea; third of sea becomes blood

3. **THIRD TRUMPET**
   Star falls on a third of rivers

4. **FOURTH TRUMPET**
   Third of sun, third of moon, third of stars turn dark

Interlude: Woe! Woe! Woe! (8:13)

5. **FIFTH TRUMPET**
   Demon locusts from the Abyss

6. **SIXTH TRUMPET**
   200 million demonic riders from the Euphrates

Interlude

The Little Scroll: Promise for the church (10:1–11)
The Two Witnesses (11:1–14)

7. **SEVENTH TRUMPET**
   "The kingdom of the world has become the
   kingdom of our Lord" (11:15).

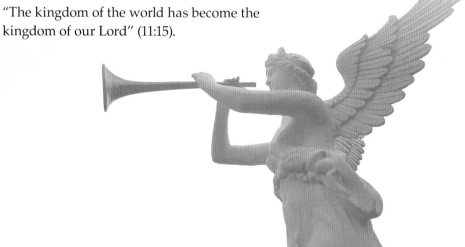

4 SEVEN SYMBOLIC HISTORIES
REVELATION 12:1–14:20

1. **HISTORY OF THE DRAGON (12:7–12)**
   Defeated
   The "ancient serpent"

2. **HISTORY OF THE WOMAN (12:13–17)**
   Persecuted by the dragon
   Defended by God

3. **THE SEA BEAST (13:1–10)**
   Ten horns and seven heads
   Blasphemer
   Has power to make war

4. **THE EARTH BEAST (13:11–18)**
   Two horns
   Deceiver
   666—the number of the beast

5. **THE 144,000 (14:1–5)**
   Marked with God's name
   Worshipers

6. **THE ANGELIC ANNOUNCERS (14:6–13)**
   First angel: "Fear God"
   Second angel: "Fallen! Fallen is Babylon the Great"
   Third angel: Warning against the mark of the beast

7. **THE HARVEST (14:14–20)**

5 SEVEN BOWLS
REVELATION 15:1–16:21

Commissioning of the Seven Angels with the Last Seven Plagues (15:1–8)

The Seven Bowls (16:1–21)

1. **FIRST BOWL**
   Painful sores

2. **SECOND BOWL**
   Turns sea into blood

3. **THIRD BOWL**
   Turns rivers and springs of water into blood

4. **FOURTH BOWL**
   Sun burns people with fire

5. **FIFTH BOWL**
   Plunges kingdom of the beast into darkness

6. **SIXTH BOWL**
   Dries up the Euphrates; Armageddon

7. **SEVENTH BOWL**
   Judgment against Babylon. "It is done!"

6 SEVEN MESSAGES OF JUDGMENT
REVELATION 17:1–19:10

Judgment Against Babylon (17:1–6)

1. **FIRST ANGELIC MESSAGE (17:7–18)**
   Explanation of the vision

2. **SECOND ANGELIC MESSAGE (18:1–3)**
   Announcement of the fall of Babylon

3. **THIRD ANGELIC MESSAGE (18:4–8)**
   Call to God's people; God's judgment on Babylon

4. **FOURTH ANGELIC MESSAGE (18:9–10)**
   Lament for the fall of Babylon by the kings of the earth

5. **FIFTH ANGELIC MESSAGE (18:11–17)**
   Lament for the fall of Babylon by the merchants of the earth

6. **SIXTH ANGELIC MESSAGE (18:18–19)**
   Lament for the fall of Babylon by the seafaring people
   Rejoice for God's judgment (18:20)

7. **SEVENTH ANGELIC MESSAGE (18:21–24)**
   Announcement of the final destruction of Babylon

Interlude

Rejoicing for Babylon's Demise (19:1–5)
Christ's Bride (19:6–10)

7 SEVEN VISIONS
REVELATION 19:11–22:5

1. **FIRST VISION (19:11–16)**
   Heaven opens and the white horse rider appears

2. **SECOND VISION (19:17–18)**
   Angel invites birds to "the great supper of God"

3. **THIRD VISION (19:19–21)**
   The beast and kings ready for war

4. **FOURTH VISION (20:1–3)**
   The thousand years (millennium)

5. **FIFTH VISION (20:4–10)**
   Thrones with judges, and Satan's doom

6. **SIXTH VISION (20:11–15)**
   Judgment of the dead

7. **SEVENTH VISION (21:1–22:5)**
   A vision of "a new heaven and a new earth"

Epilogue (22:6–21)

Jesus is coming back: "Amen. Come, Lord Jesus!"

PHOTOS AND ILLUSTRATIONS

Images used under license from Shutterstock.com: Nils Prause, cover; muratart, cover; Gaman Mihai-Radu, cover; ronstik, cover, p. 12; Andres Sonne pp. 5, 69, 131; jorisvo p. 8; Marcin Krzyzak p. 15; Cortyn p. 22; dinosmichail pp. 29, 91; Yasonya p. 31; Oleksii Liebiediev p. 34; Ben Photo p. 37; Izabela Miszczak p. 41; mythja p. 43; dogusoz p. 44; Liliya Butenko p. 47; Nataliya Nazarova p. 49; Stefan Holm p. 52; Lefteris Papaulakis p. 54; Marco Ramerini p. 59, 111; BRAIN2HANDS p. 62; Viliam.M p. 65; James the Just in Church of the Holy Trinity, Corfu, Greece, photo by Storm Is Me p. 73; Rafal Redelowski p. 74; Renata Sedmakova: St. John the Evangelist from mosaic of Immaculate Conception in Pfarrkirche Kaisermuhlen, Vienna, Austria, p. 80, fresco of St. John the Evangelist in Cathedral of Saint Giovanni Battista, Turin, Italy p. 101, fresco of St. Mark in Rosenkranz Basilica, Berlin, Germany p. 102, statue of the apostle Paul, Paris, France p. 103, fresco of Jesus giving peter the keys in Chiesa di Santa Maria in Transpontina and chapel of St. Peter and Paul, Rome, Italy p. 104; LifeCollectionPhotography p. 85; irena iris szewczyk p. 87; Zvonimir Atletic p. 94, fresco of St. Paul at the home of Priscilla and Aquila in the basilica of Saint Paul, Rome, Italy p. 105, fresco of Paul and Silas whipped, Rome, Italy p. 106; Mazur Travel p. 96, 97; St. James in stained glass, Panaspics p. 100; BearFotos p. 114; garanga p.115; Nejdet Duzen p. 116, 124; OPIS Zagreb p. 117; cedinsel p. 119; AHMETOZER35 p. 121; Nurten erdal p. 122; tomertu p. 125; godongphoto p. 125; n_defender p. 126; John Copland p. 127; Heiner Weiss p. 127; Andriy Kananovych p. 128; Vivida Photo PC p. 128; Garsya p. 133; sondem p. 133; Ververidis Vasilis p. 134; sebra p. 134; Limages Studio p. 144; Burdun Iliya p. 145; wk1003mike p. 146; Francesca Tomba p. 147; jessicahyde p. 148; Zolnierek p. 149; Philip Steury Photography p. 150.

Image used under license from iStock: aluxum p. 74.

Other images: Patmos mosaic, Wikimedia Commons/Njaker p. 9; Andronicus and Junia, Wikimedia Commons/Asia p. 92; Aristarchus of Thessalonica, Wikimedia Commons/Andrija12345678 p. 93; Timothy, Wikimedia Commons/Andreas F. Borchert p. 107; King Eumenes II, Wikimedia Commons/Sailko p. 107; Mural depicting Revelation 3 in Cathedral of the Immaculate Conception, Tepic, Mexico, Wikimedia Commons/Nheyob p. 132.

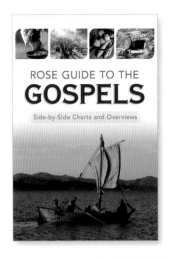

ROSE GUIDE TO THE GOSPELS

Includes: key information about the uniqueness of each gospel; a harmony of the gospels; who's who in the gospels; background to the world of Jesus; evidence for the resurrection; and more.

ISBN 9781628628111

ROSE GUIDE TO THE BOOK OF ACTS

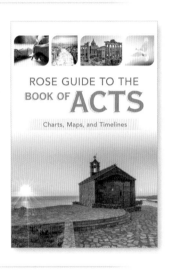

Includes: overview of the book of Acts; understanding the message and background of Acts; life of the apostle Paul; who's who in Acts; time line and maps; the Holy Spirit in the lives of Christians; and more.

ISBN 9781649380203

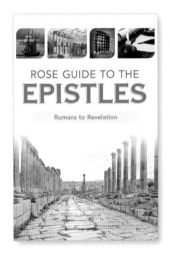

ROSE GUIDE TO THE EPISTLES

Includes: overview of the epistles; key facts on each epistle at a glance; who's who in the epistles; the seven churches of Revelation; comparison of Christian views on the book of Revelation; and more.

ISBN 9781649380227

www.hendricksonrose.com